This is the story of the flying bomb (doodlebug and rocket) attacks on Great Britain as it has never been told before. A wealth of photographs, maps and diagrams alongside stories of tragedy, endurance and courage help to recreate the atmosphere of life as it was in those remarkable days between June, 1944 and March, 1945. The work of the Royal Observer Corps, Civil Defence, the fire, police and ambulance services, the men on the anti-aircraft guns, the ATS, the boys and girls of Balloon Command and the "women in green" (WVS) is told in detail. So, also, is the role of the RAF who played their part by photographing and bombing the launching sites and then meeting and repulsing the foe in this new Battle of London.

DOODLEBUGS *and* ROCKETS

The Battle of the Flying Bombs

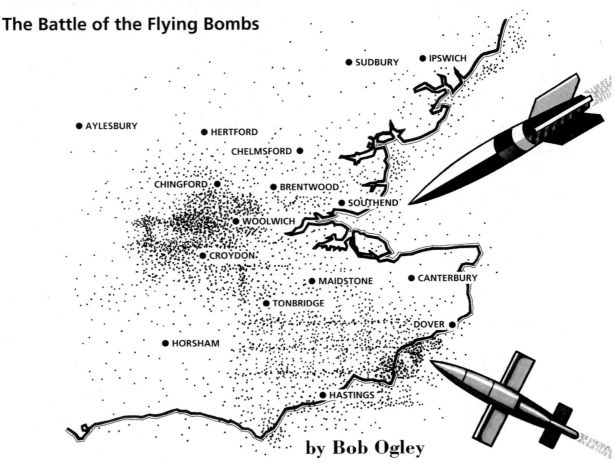

by Bob Ogley

Froglets Publications

Froglets Publications

Brasted Chart, Westerham,
Kent, TN16 1LY

Tel: 01959 562972
Fax: 01959 565365

© Bob Ogley 1992

ISBN 1 872337 22 8 (Casebound)
ISBN 1 872337 21 X (Paperback)

Front Cover shows a Tempest V, piloted by Squadron Leader Roland Beamont chasing a V1 flying bomb above the Kentish countryside in the summer of 1944 painted by Geoffrey Nutkins, Shoreham Air Historical Museum, High Street, Shoreham. (by courtesy of Group Captain Hugh Tudor)

Back Cover: The Battle of London painted by Frank Salisbury. by courtesy of Mr Julian Sandys

This book was originated by Froglets Publications Ltd and printed and bound by Thanet Press Ltd, Margate, Kent. A catalogue record for this book is available from the British Library.

Jacket design by Alison Stammers

**First published September 1992
Reprinted November 1992, July 1994
and May 1995**

Acknowledgements and Credits

THE flying bomb was a unique, brilliantly conceived, indiscriminate and short-lived weapon that was launched by the Germans in a last-ditch orgy of terror, designed to turn the tide of war. The main thrust of the V1 campaign began on June 12, 1944 and lasted only ten weeks. It was followed by the V2, the rocket projectile that brought a new dimension to air warfare, and cast a shadow that still hangs over the world today. By March, 1945 when the last missile appeared out of the stratosphere and crashed onto the town of Orpington, the war had virtually been won by the Allies and history was being made in almost every corner of the globe.

The flying bomb campaign, then overshadowed by events and of no real military significance, was largely ignored by historians until the writer, Norman Longmate, with an enormous wealth of official material which had been denied to earlier historians because of the "thirty year rule", published his books *The Doodlebugs* and *Hitler's Rockets* — two full investigations into the concept, development and subsequent effects of the flying bomb menace.

Mr Longmate discovered that the V1 and V2, short-lived as they were, made an extraordinary and lasting impact on all who lived in Southern England in 1944 and 1945. I have had the same reaction. Appealing in the local press for reminiscences and photographs, I was overwhelmed by the response. Hundreds of letters, scores and scores of telephone calls and many stirring stories from those I casually met in the street. Thousands of people remember the Doodlebugs and Rockets. It's not surprising -- everyone living in southern and eastern England at the time was on the receiving end.

This book is not intended to be a military history or a full account of the great intelligence hunt but an attempt to recreate the atmosphere of life as it was at the time using photographs and maps from newspapers, museums, libraries and private sources -- many of which have never been published before. Interwoven with these is a brief history and some of the more fascinating anecdotes and letters. The picture is completed by contemporary documents and statistics and colour photographs of some of those who "played a leading part".

I am grateful for the professional help I received from local newspapers, particularly the *Kent Messenger* whose photographic archives have been preserved with great care. I have used more than 30 pictures taken in Kent in 1944 or 1945, the locations of which could not be named in the newspaper at the time because of the censorship policy which then applied. This book could not have been written without the co-operation of those who printed my appeal for reminiscences and those who responded.

In May 1945, Winston Churchill said: "The lights went out and the bombs came down. But every man, woman and child in the country had no thought of quitting the struggle." I hope that all those who experienced the flying bombs, those who missed them by virtue of being elsewhere and the young people who have inherited an enormous interest in the war years will find something in these pages to remind them that we didn't quit, despite the late arrival on the scene of Hitler's miracle weapons.

Photographs in this book are the copyright of the following: Kent Messenger Newspapers: pages 28, 29, 43, 46, 47, 54, 60, 62, 69, 70, 80, 81, 98, 99, 101,105, 109,111, 113, 114,116, 118, 121, 122, 124, 126, 127,128,132-133, 145, 152, 153,155, 160, 162, 183,182top, 191.192. Imperial War Museum 4, 7, 11, 12, 14, 17, 22, 25, 36, 37, 40, 41, 42, 44, 49, 53, 56, 57, 72, 73, 76, 77,82, 84, 85, 88R, 94, 106, 107R, 115,119, 120, 123,129, 140, 151, 156, 161, 163, 176, 177, 180, 186, 187, 188, 189. Deutsches Museum, München 6, 8, 9, 10, 18, 27, 139, 203. Towner Art Gallery, Eastbourne 38, 117: Topham Picture Agency 35, 39, 58, 79, 158, 159, 165, 171, 185. Railway Museum 31. R.V. Jones 20. RAF Biggin Hill 45L. Bromley Library 63, 71, 172. Croydon Library (Croydon Advertiser) 65, 67, 68, 100. Beckett Newspapers, Hastings 74. East Grinstead History Museum 86. London Fire Brigade 91, 142. Newham Library 90. Syndication International 96. Kentish Mercury (Lewisham Local Studies) 103. The Ted Carter Collection (Waltham Abbey Historical Society) 146, 178. Bexley Local History Studies 147, Southend Library 154. Fern Flynn 97, 102, 125, 195, 198, 199, 202, 207. Other photographs come from private, individual sources. Artwork by Alison Stammers.

A special thank you to Jill Goldsworthy who helped with the research and the typesetting and was greatly involved with the production at all stages.

THE CONTENTS

Various maps, charts, diagrams and statistics which may be helpful in following the story of the flying bomb campaign are contained on the following pages:

A special section in colour appears between pages 193 and 208

The V1 was a pilotless mid-wing monoplane, 25 ft 4 in long, constructed of plywood and sheet steel. Its wing span was 17 ft 6 in and it was propelled by a pulse-jet engine. The direction of the bomb was governed automatically by a gyroscopic unit that gave signals to the air-operated rudder and elevator which stabilised it. Directional information was obtained from a pre-set compass. An air-log measured the pre-set distance after which the elevators were depressed and the robot dived to the ground. The nose was armed with 850 kg of high explosive, bolted to the forward end of the fuel tank.

INTRODUCTION

V for Vengeance

ON June 6, 1944, only a few hours after the D Day landings, the German High Command gave orders for an immediate assault on Britain. Six days later the first of the new Vengeance Weapons made its appearance. This was the V1 or *Vergeltungswaffe 1*, better known to Londoners and those in south-east England as the flying bomb or "doodlebug".

The V1 was launched on a country still showing terrible scars from the 1940-41 blitz. It was a novel but deadly weapon, a pilotless mid-wing monoplane armed with an explosive nose and propelled by a pulse-jet engine. Coming directly after D Day, when everyone in England thought the war was almost won, it had a devastating effect on morale. During the summer of 1944 several thousand missiles landed in southern England killing almost 5,500 civilians and inflicting enormous damage to property in London and the Home Counties.

Day after day, night after night, the ungainly monsters, would speed across the skies, sometimes just above rooftop height. Resembling a wooden cross in the sky and spitting red flames from its tail, the missile made a noise like a badly-tuned motorbike engine that became louder and louder as it approached. To the people below it was a once-heard-never-forgotten sound as it clattered along on its deadly mission towards the capital. When the engine cut out the missile would fall silently to earth followed, several seconds later, by an ear-shattering explosion.

The loss of life in London, was considerable. 121 died in the middle of a morning service in the Guards Chapel, 48 died when a bomb fell in The Aldwych and 74 were killed when the US Army billets in Sloane Court, Chelsea received a direct hit. It was the London Civil Defence Region which bore the brunt of the assault. The 2,419 V1's which dropped in the London boroughs killed 5,126 people. Outside London, 2,789 flying bombs caused another 350 deaths. In terms of casualties the "doodlebugs" were worse than the Blitz.

In the face of this German offensive the defences in England were strengthened immediately. Anti-aircraft guns and barrage balloons were massed on the approaches to London and fighter aircraft patrolled an outer defensive screen. Between them they destroyed

Between June 13, 1944 and March 29, 1945 a total of 9,251 V1 flying bombs were plotted. Of these 2,419 reached London. The total number destroyed was 4,261 — 1,971 by anti-aircraft, 1,979 by the Royal Air Force, 278 by balloons and 33 by the Royal Navy

many V1's, gradually gained the upper hand and the threat diminished.

But Hitler had another, more deadly, revenge weapon. This was the long-range rocket, known as the V2, which flew at around 3,600 miles an hour and arrived without warning via the stratosphere. It was 46 feet long with four stabilising fins, a cylindrical body and a warhead of one ton. The V2 took just five minutes from launch to impact and travelled too high and too fast to be tracked down. There was no time to give an anti-aircraft warning. It was a weapon with which Hitler could have won the war.

From September 1944 to March 1945, 1,115 V2 rockets were fired at Britain killing 2,612 people in London and 212 civilians elsewhere. London received 517 rockets and 537 fell outside the capital, the remainder in the sea. Many more rockets were destined to land on British soil but the Allied armies gained the initiative, the launching sites and rocket pads were overrun and, late in March 1945, the ordeal came to an end.

With the V1 and V2 Hitler brought the war to Britain as the Luftwaffe had done in 1940 and German Minister of Propaganda, Dr Josef Goebbels boasted of the great destruction of London. But Londoners and others throughout the south-east faced the onslaught with courage and with a defiance that was, by 1944, their hallmark.

Those who lived through the summer and autumn of 1944 and the winters of 1944 and '45 will never forget the Vengeance Weapons. Many loved ones lie in communal graves, beneath headstones on which are inscribed the words 'By enemy action', and others still bear the scars of injury. Thousands of families, who lost precious possessions when their homes were destroyed, can look back with a slender slice of comfort — the battle of the flying bomb was a victory for the Allies. Victory at a price.

CHAPTER 1: SECRET WEAPONS

"There are serious indications that Germany has been developing bacterial warfare, gases, flame weapons, glider bombs and pilotless aircraft, and long range guns, and it is recommended that necessary precautions be taken".

Dr R.V. Jones, November, 1939

As a scientific adviser to the Air Ministry, Dr R.V. Jones was the man responsible for the early investigations into the feasibility of "secret weapons" in Germany. In November, 1939 he completed a report for the Secret Intelligence Services with this sombre warning. He was right. The Germans had been designing novel weapons including a long range guided missile which had been on the drawing board since 1930. Photograph shows one of the earliest research rockets, the Winkler HWZ. Test firing took place in 1931 on the small island of Greifswalder Oie in the Baltic Sea.

A national joke

Sleeping beauty

Rocket age arrives

Operation Cherrystone

The "Wunderwaffe"

Mid-summer photocalls

Raid on Peenemunde

The "ski sites"

No-ball assault

Sinister activities

A national joke

IT was Adolf Hitler in one of his hysterical broadcasts who first mentioned the existence in Germany of a secret weapon. The war was little more than two weeks old when the Führer spoke in the city of Danzig on Tuesday September 19, 1939. He reflected: "The moment might very quickly come for us to use a weapon with which we ourselves could not be attacked".

In Britain, Hitler's "secret weapon" made headlines everywhere and the Secret Intelligence Services (SIS) with headquarters in Broadway, London were instructed to find out more. After painstaking investigations through SIS files, Dr R.V. Jones, a scientific adviser to the Air Ministry, came up with these conclusions: "There are a number of weapons to which general references occur, and of which some must be considered seriously. They include — bacterial warfare, new gases, flame weapons, gliding bombs, aerial torpedoes and pilotless aircraft, long range guns and rockets, new torpedoes, mines and submarines, death rays, engine-stopping rays and magnetic guns."

As the weeks passed by there was no sign of the "secret weapon" and it became a national joke, dismissed by newspapers as German bluff, possibly by the Propaganda Minister, Dr Joseph Goebbels.

It was no bluff at all. For many years, German scientists had been designing two novel weapons. One was a pilotless jet-propelled aircraft; the other was a long-range guided missile — a sophisticated and brilliant conception that had been on the drawing boards since 1930 and was known as the *Aggregat 1* or *A1*.

Director of the rocket programme was Walter Dornberger, an artillery officer in the German Army, the Wehrmacht, which, by the Treaty of Versailles, had been limited to just 10,000 men. Dornberger's assistant from 1932 was Werner von Braun, a young scientist with a passion for rocketry and space exploration. The two men worked at the Army Weapons Department at Kummersdorf, just south of Berlin.

By 1932 the *A1* was designed and built but plagued by considerable teething troubles which Dornberger sought to solve while von Braun, with an independent team, developed another rocket, the liquid-filled *A2*, stabilised by gyro-mechanism and capable of reaching an altitude of 7,000 feet.

In 1933 Adolf Hitler gained control of the German Government and became the Führer of the Third Reich. Although he was not greatly enthusiastic about the rocket programme — he considered it to be little more than an elaborate toy — he was nonetheless

Dr Josef Goebbels, with a Nazi party armband and Adolf Hitler on the Führer's 55th birthday, April 20, 1944

anxious that it should be developed in the strictest secrecy. As von Braun began work on an even larger and heavier missile, the *A3*, it became clear that Kummersdorf was too large, too heavily populated with too many prying eyes for the testing of such a weapon. Another site would have to be found.

In 1935, von Braun, now 27 years old, visited the island of Usedom on the Baltic sea where his father used to shoot ducks. He considered it the perfect place for guided missile tests. Walter Dornberger agreed and recommended that the northern peninsular of the island be purchased immediately.

Within 12 months the new rocket base was taking shape close to a small fishing village called Peenemunde.

The A4 rocket is towed into position and erected by a Meiller trailer next to the inspection platform. Many of the early launch attempts failed but a thorough investigation of these failures led to constant improvements in performance, and on October 3, 1942 the breakthrough success was attained.

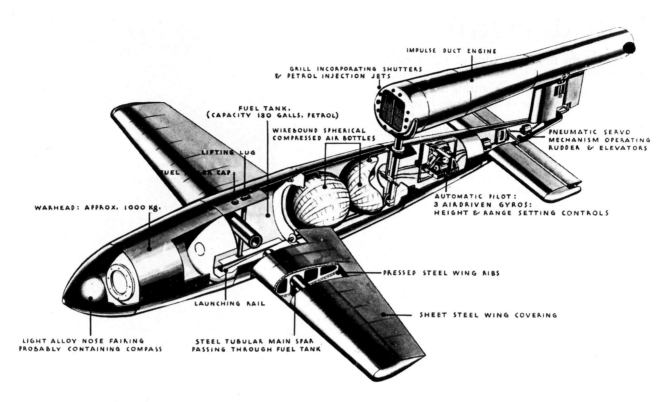

IMPULSE DUCT ENGINE

GRILL INCORPORATING SHUTTERS & PETROL INJECTION JETS

FUEL TANK, (CAPACITY 130 GALLS, PETROL)

WIREBOUND SPHERICAL COMPRESSED AIR BOTTLES

LIFTING LUG

FUEL TANK CAP.

WARHEAD: APPROX. 1000 Kg.

PNEUMATIC SERVO MECHANISM OPERATING RUDDER & ELEVATORS

AUTOMATIC PILOT: 3 AIRDRIVEN GYROS: HEIGHT & RANGE SETTING CONTROLS

PRESSED STEEL WING RIBS

SHEET STEEL WING COVERING

LAUNCHING RAIL

LIGHT ALLOY NOSE FAIRING PROBABLY CONTAINING COMPASS

STEEL TUBULAR MAIN SPAR PASSING THROUGH FUEL TANK

Operation Cherrystone

AS the German Army continued to test-fire and perfect the *A4* rocket, the Luftwaffe were by no means idle in the business of weapon development. Forced on the defensive by the Battle of Britain and then by the opening salvoes in the offensives against their cities, they were keen to retaliate and any restraints on using indiscriminate weapons against civilians were rapidly disappearing.

The opportunity came in March, 1942 when the Argus Motorenwerke Company asked the Air Ministry in Berlin if it were still interested in pilotless aircraft — a project that had been on the drawing boards just before the outbreak of war. The idea appealed to Field Marshal Erhard Milch, deputy to Reichsmarshal Hermann Goering, Commander-in-Chief of the Luftwaffe. On May 28, 1942, Milch met Robert Lusser, an aircraft designer and outlined his plan for an Argus-tube-propelled pilotless missile.

Lusser's designs met Milch's needs to perfection. It would make no demand on the aluminium industry, being made of thin steel plate, it would burn low-grade petrol instead of scarce and costly high-octane aviation spirit and the labour would be extremely small, only 550 man hours per robot — excluding the explosive and auto-pilot.

The idea of a flying bomb became a firm project on June 9, 1942. Fieseler Flugzeugbau, makers of the 196 or Storch, a small high-wing monoplane powered by an Argus engine, received specifications of the new aircraft which, they were told, should be able to carry a warhead of around 200 lbs and was to be driven by a pulse-jet engine. The project was code-named *"Kirschkern,"* or *"Cherrystone"*.

On July 19, 1942 representatives of Argus and Fieseler met Milch in Berlin where the decision was made to go straight into production as soon as the development work was completed. The designation, Fieseler Fi 103 was adopted and the date given was the end of 1943.

High above the clouds, this Mosquito of 540 Squadron, based at Leuchars on the east coast of Scotland, was on its way to photograph Peenemunde. Reconnaissance pictures became a vital part of RAF operational work in the bid to solve the mystery of the "secret weapons". Hour after hour, day after day, airmen of the service reconnaissance units flew their Mosquitoes over the North Sea and then on to Peenemunde.

ON April 20, 1943 Mr Duncan Sandys was officially appointed by the Prime Minister to head the *Bodyline* Committee (later to become *Crossbow*) and review the evidence for German long-range rocket development. His appointment met with a hostile reaction from Lord Cherwell (formerly Professor Lindemann), the Prime Minister's Scientific Advisor, who wanted Dr Jones, as a scientist, to direct the inquiry. Cherwell considered that such devices could not be fired over long ranges with any degree of accuracy and dismissed the rocket notion as "fantastic" and "unreal." He persued a trenchant campaign for Mr Sandys removal as Britain's supremo in the hunt for rocket clues.

Mr Sandys and his military advisor, Colonel Kenneth Post, stuck to their task, initiating numerous photographic missions over Peenemunde and France, working closely with the interpreters at Medmenham, and making inspection tours of Normandy.

In November 1943, Mr Sandys' responsibilities were transferred to the Deputy Chief of Air Staff and a Joint Intelligence Sub-Committee was instructed to initiate counter measures against pilotless aircraft, which by now had been indentified. With his retirement from the scene, the rocket inquiry, for which there was still much scepticism at high level, lost its momentum.

A few days after the V1 offensive began, on June 19, 1944, Duncan Sandys returned to the fray to chair the *Crossbow* Committee, with even wider powers to co-ordinate British counter measures.

Peenemunde — the photograph taken in June, 1943 on which A4 rockets were first recognised. General Dornberger later confirmed this 'test stand' as the one from which the first successful launching of the A4 took place.

The raid on Peenemunde

BOMBER Command received orders to attack three separate areas of Peenemunde in what was to be the only operation of the war in which the entire force was employed at night. The Air Ministry made it clear to Sir Arthur Harris, Commander-in-Chief of Bomber Command, that the idea of the raid was to destroy the workshops and laboratories where the missile was designed and assembled, and kill or incapacitate as many scientists or technicians as possible, by bombing their sleeping quarters. There were no instructions to attack the airfield at Peenemunde West, or the large camp for foreign workers.

The rocket site was 500 miles from Britain — a difficult, almost impossible target for the Army or Navy — but well within range for the squadrons of Bomber Command, whose men had never heard of Peenemunde and had no idea of its great threat to the civilian population and the Allies' prospects of invading Europe.

The operation had to wait several weeks for suitable weather conditions — a full, or nearly full moon with no cloud over Peenemunde, was essential. The forecasters recommended Tuesday August 17, 1943 and on the afternoon of that historic day final orders were issued to the Main Force of Bomber Command. Of the 58 squadrons, 54 were to go into action that night in an operation code-named *Hydra*. A diversionary attack on Berlin by a few Mosquito Pathfinders to decoy the Luftwaffe night fighters was code-named *Whitebait*.

The route chosen for the bombers was over the North Sea, Denmark and the Baltic Sea. It was to be a high-explosive raid using a Master Bomber who would remain in the target area throughout the raid to radio advice to his Pathfinders and then to the Main Force. The tactics also included a "timed run" on a fixed bearing from a known position.

The Master Bomber technique had been pioneered by Guy Gibson VC on a raid of the Ruhr Dams. The dangerous but highly responsible task on this occasion was to go to Group Captain John Searby commanding 83 Squadron. Two deputy master bombers were selected in case Searby was shot down. The briefing took place with neither the briefers nor aircrew knowing what there was at Peenemunde but they were told that the work on the base was so important that the raid would have to be repeated night after night until the site was razed to the ground.

Some hours later, 596 bombers carrying 1,650 tons of high explosive and 274 tons of incendiaries set off across the North Sea on what was to be the only precision raid undertaken by the RAF at night during the whole of the second world war. It was to be a night of action and drama with many lives lost.

The first bomber to take off was a Stirling of 90 Squadron based at West Wickham, Cambridgeshire, piloted by Flight Lieutenant George Crew. Behind him were 324 Lancasters, 218 Halifax's and 53 Stirlings, each squadron taking a different path across the North Sea to the point marked on the navigators' map as Position A.

A few hours later Peenemunde was burning. The raid was considered by the RAF to be a huge success. At least 25 buildings which formed the Experimental Works — the scientific heart of Peenemunde — were destroyed, including the headquarters office block and the design office. There were direct hits on the assembly buildings where the V2 rocket was about to be mass produced. Valuable documents were destroyed and Dr Walter Thiel, engineer responsible for the rocket propulsion department, was killed.

Tragically many bombs fell in the area which contained the camp for foreign workers; very few were allowed to take shelter and the death toll was appalling — more than 600 Polish labourers or Russian prisoners of war.   In another area a large dormitory building, occupied by young women, was destroyed by blast and there was great loss of life. Some of the girls, forced out of the building by fire or terror, were killed while running to the beach.

Apart from Herr Thiel most of the leading German scientists survived including Walter Dornberger and Werner von Braun, who courageously rescued many of his documents from the flames. According to the Germans few items of scientific importance were lost. However, one objective of the raid was to delay the production of the V2 rocket and this was achieved.

It was decided not to rebuild Peenemunde immediately and the base was left with a deliberately damaged appearance. The test-firing of rockets was moved to Poland and mass production to underground caves.

So ended the raid on Peenemunde -- a mission that had nothing to do with the Vl for the British did not know of the link between the Flying Bomb and Peenemunde until after the operation. Many stray bombs fell well beyond the area selected for attack but, ironically, the airfield at Peenemunde West where the Flying Bomb tests were carried out did not receive a single hit.

Dr Jones was not consulted about the aiming points in the raid but, in retrospect, he wished he had been. Bomber Command had originally intended to make its main attack on the development works and installation at Peenemunde but Duncan Sandys convinced the Command that it was even more important to attack the housing estate where the scientists lived.

"I would probably not have agreed", said Dr Jones, "because the main emphasis should have been to smash up the research and manufacturing facilities. But with the emphasis on the housing estate, a substantial portion of our bombs fell to the south of the establishment itself, and particularly on the camp which housed the foreign labourers, including those who had risked so much to get information through to us. We never had another report from them and some 600 of them were killed compared with 130 or so German scientists, engineers and other staff. On the debit side there was the fact that we lost 41 aircraft out of 596."

How much vital production time did the Germans lose by the British raid on their military experimental site at Peenemunde? Six months, or more, said General Eisenhower. At least two months, said Dr Jones. Six to eight weeks, said Dr Joseph Goebbels. Two months, say the official British history books.

Master bomber, Group Captain John Searby of 83 Squadron who remained in the target area throughout the raid on Peenemunde

A view of the Karlshagen community after the raid on Peenemunde. Most of these houses were occupied by scientists or engineers.

The "ski site" at Bois Carré, near Yvrench — the first V1 launching site in France to be analysed on photographs This one was taken on November 9, 1943 and shows the long. low building of heavy concrete which was used for the storage of flying bomb components. Within a few weeks, similar constructions were identified on photographs between Dieppe and Calais.

Launch pads and "ski sites"

JUST before the raid on Peenemunde a new suspicious construction site was discovered on reconnaissance photographs taken in the Pas de Calais area, near St Omer.

The site was hidden in Foret d'Eperlecques at Watten and, although no-one at the time knew what its purpose would be, instructions were given to the US Eighth Air Force to bomb it.

It was later discovered that the Germans were building a bomb-proof concrete launch pad for the V2 rocket and the Americans' daylight attack on August 27, 1943 so thoroughly smashed it up that the project had to be abandoned. In its place the Germans built a massive bomb-proof concrete factory for the manufacture of the liquid oxygen needed to fuel the rockets.

A few weeks later, in November, another "suspicious erection" was discovered on a new set of photographs. These showed a long, low building with a curved end and was christened "ski site" by photographic interpreters. Again, no-one knew for what purpose it would be used but orders were issued to destroy it.

Crossbow and the No-Ball assault

One of the many problems facing British Intelligence was to discover a coherent theme running through the information coming in from France, Poland and elsewhere, for many agents were confusing the rocket with the pilotless aircraft. On September 3, 1943 one agent, known simply as "Amniarix", managed to send through a remarkably detailed account of the "stratospheric bomb tests" which contained information also of Colonel Wachtel's regiments and the "catapult sites". Dr Jones tried to find the source of this valuable new information but was only told it came from a young girl. After the war the secret was unveiled. Jeanne Rousseau, aged 23, was "Agent Amniarix". She spoke five languages and worked as an interpreter. In 1976, Yorkshire Television traced her and arranged for Dr Jones to meet her for the first time (see picture). Jeanne was now Vicomtesse de Clarens.

THE massive jigsaw, presented piece by piece to military intelligence from agents on the ground was still not fully taking shape, but early in November, 1943 came a new twist in the chain of events. A contact working at a building site in the Abbeville district of France, noticed "a different type of construction". Camera-equipped Mosquitoes confirmed it was something a little under 300 feet in length and from the air looked "like a ski site".

More photographic sorties were made; in fact the whole area of north-west France within 150 miles of London was subject to the most careful scrutiny and thousands of pictures were taken. By November 22, 95 ski sites had been positively identified but no-one could be certain for what sinister purpose they would be used. It was now obvious that these sites, more than 250 feet long and 10 feet wide, were connected with Hitler's most-vaunted secret weapons, but were they launching sites for glider bombs, pilotless aircraft or long-range rockets?

On November 28, 1943 a new set of photographs of Peenemunde was taken by Squadron Leader Merifield. They appeared to show little that was new but Flight Officer Constance Babington Smith, a young WAAF officer who specialised in enemy aircraft recognition, compared the new set of prints with previous photographs of the same area. She noticed a sort of ramp banked up with earth, supporting rails that inclined towards the water's edge. She reported her find to Wing Commander Douglas Kendall, the interpreter in charge of the investigation.

"Don't you think it might be a catapult for pilotless aircraft?" Kendall replied: "Babs, I know it is". On another photograph her trained eye fastened onto a tiny cruciform shape, set exactly on the lower end of the inclined rails — a midget aircraft actually in place for launching. It was an observation that was to earn her a place in history. Flight Officer Babington Smith had made the first British sighting of a flying bomb.

Before daylight the next morning Wing Commander Kendall's report report was on its way to London with the news that the most imminent cross-Channel threat was established beyond doubt. It was going to be a flying bomb. At this point it seemed that the attacks, when they came, would be of an appalling magnitude. The ski-buildings provided storage space for 20 flying bombs, and as there were nearly 100 sites, it seemed likely that something like 2,000 bombs would be launched each day.

Britain's secret weapon inquiry, codenamed *Bodyline*, was replaced

Wing Commander Leonard Cheshire, commanding 617 (Dambusters) Squadron led the first serious attack on the No-Ball sites on the night of December 16, 1943. The target was near Abbeville and was marked by Mosquitos of the Pathfinder Force. Cheshire, leading the main force of nine Lancasters, delivered the bombs within 150 feet of the markers. Two were actually within 90 feet, but it was still not close enough to destroy the site. In later sorties Cheshire's low-level marking technique, flying Mosquitos and Mustangs, made pin-point attacks possible. For his outstanding and extensive period of operational low-level flying in the most dangerous circumstances, Leonard Cheshire was later to be awarded the Victoria Cross.

by *Crossbow*; the ski sites, now a target for Fighter Command, were called *No-Ball* sites and orders were issued to eliminate them forthwith. Fighters alone, however, could not destroy the massive concrete buildings, now spreading rapidly across northern France, so reinforcements were introduced. Heavy bombers of the recently-established Allied Expeditionary Air Force, supported by bombers of the US Air Force, joined the *No-Ball* counter attack. The Americans were ordered "to get the job done in days, not weeks". It was not that easy. The novelist, H.E.Bates, then working in the Public Relations Department of the Air Ministry wrote:

"Such small targets demanded a far greater degree of accuracy than was needed to knock out a factory. The Germans' favourite site was a small wood of five to ten acres close to a hard road, where trees in both summer and winter gave them perfect cover. In such woodland sites the Germans built hundreds of sites and supply depots. But they also chose more domestic sites. Orchards of apples and pears were favourite places. Nor had they any compunction whatsoever about putting them in the back gardens of French peasants in remote villages. And on at least one occasion they built an entire launching site in a village street."

Bombing was dangerous and wildly inaccurate. On Christmas Eve, a year after the first successful flying bomb test, 672 American Fortresses attacked 24 separate sites. Other attacks that day brought the number involved to 1,300 — the largest single operation ever undertaken by the US Eighth Air Force. The results were disappointing. By the end of December only seven sites had been destroyed and the Germans were still completing new sites faster than the Allies could destroy them.

The New Year proved more successful but defences were strong and losses heavy. In one attack alone, near Cherbourg, 160 out of 217 Marauders were damaged by flak. By the end of May, 1944, 82 *No-Ball* sites were believed to have been neutralised but the Allies had lost 154 aircraft and 771 aircrew were dead or missing. This included 48 heavy bombers and 462 men of the US Eighth Air Force. There were other victims of the *Crossbow* campaign. Some sites had attracted as many as 4,000 bombs and the countryside around them was bleak with tragedy.

H.E.Bates, who visited the Pas de Calais, wrote: "Its villages have crumbled into heaps of stone and plaster; its fields are like miniature alpine ranges....village streets are chains of ponds after heavy rain, gardens and orchards have been obliterated. For the night and day bombing which caused all this, the French had a single and terribly expressive word — 'Effrayant!' Yet again and again the observer talking to them in the days immediately after their liberation heard them say: 'We did not mind....however often you came and however much you bombed us. We knew it had to be done and that it had to be done to us'. "

An air reconnaissance photograph of part of the experimental station at Peenemunde taken on November 28, 1943 by Squadron Leader John Merifield (inset). It shows a launching ramp on which, less than three weeks later, the trained eye of Constance Babington Smith who worked at the Photographic Interpretation Unit at Danesfield Medmenham, detected a miniature aeroplane at the end of the ramp, in position for launching. Hitler's secret was out.

Sinister activities

FLIGHT Officer Constance Babington Smith, the young WAAF who first identified the photograph of a "midget aircraft" sitting on its launching ramp at Peenemunde, was a girl who came from a background of firm dedication to her country. She was the daughter of Sir Henry Babington Smith, former private secretary to the Viceroy of India, and fiercely proud of the part being played by photographic intelligence in analysing and assessing the threat of V-weapons.

It was in May 1942 that Constance, as a photographic interpreter, flipped through a stack of pictures taken by Flight Lieutenant D.W. Steventon. Something unusual caught her eye — a collection of circular embankments at a place called Peenemunde. No-one knew what they could possibly be so the photographs were placed in the print library at Medmenham for possible future reference.

A year later with the "secret weapon" threat out in the open, Constance remembered the mysterious rings. More photographs were taken of Peenemunde and, on the evidence these provided, Operation Bodyline was established.

The Interpretation Unit at Medmenham buzzed with activity. Mr Sandys had ordered that the whole area of north-west France within 150 miles of London should be photographed — and there were hundreds of separate sorties, yielding thousands of pictures. Box files stacked up in mountains, the interpretation team worked long hours and almost every day there were sinister new activities to be examined.

It was later in 1943, months after the raid on Peenemunde, that Miss Babington Smith made her two greatest discoveries. One was a midget aircraft, smaller than a fighter, sitting in a small enclosure. The other was a sort of ramp, banked up with earth, supporting rails that inclined upwards.

With the agents who risked their lives in Germany and the occupied countries, the interrogators who questioned the prisoners of war, the men and women who combed through trade magazines and monitored German broadcasts, the technical wizards, the airmen of photographic reconnaissance and the intelligence experts, the interpreters were only part of the huge team involved in this great, often frustrating, hunt.

The vigilance of Constance Babington Smith and her colleagues contributed to the ultimate success of the Allied cause.

The photograph of the flying bomb on the launching ramp (left), interpreted by Constance Babington Smith, provided the link between Peenemunde and the launching sites in France and finally proved that the "ski sites" were for launching flying bombs.

Wing Commander Douglas Kendall, expert photographic interpreter. From 1943 onwards he co-ordinated the work on the V weapons at RAF Medmenham

23

CHAPTER 2: THE DOODLEBUGS

"After months of waiting the time has come for us to open fire. Today your wait and your work will have their reward. The order to open fire has been issued. Now that our enemy is trying to secure at all costs his foothold on the Continent, we approach our task supremely confident in our weapons; as we launch them today, and in the future let us always bear in mind the destruction and the suffering wrought by the enemy's terror bombing."

Col Max Wachtel to his Flak Regiment 155 (W) on June 12, 1944

Colonel Max Wachtel, Commanding Officer of Flak Regiment 155 (W). In the 1914-18 war, Wachtel had been an artillery officer. He rejoined the army in 1936 and eventually became commander of technical development projects and later the Anti-Aircraft Artillery School.

V1 launching site

Order to attack

Allied Landings

Diver, Diver, Diver !

Battle of London

Falling like flies

Flaming tails

At the end of April, 1944, the interpreters at Medmenham spotted a totally new development — a long concrete platform with a pair of studs embedded between it. This was a much simpler launching arrangement, labelled by Wing Commander Kendall as a "modified site". As reconnaissance work continued, Kendall put more interpreters on duty. Picture shows a Mosquito photographer returning with yet another set of photographs for the Crossbow jigsaw.

Modified sites

THE Nazis were now confident that flying bombs would provide them with a chance to snatch victory out of the jaws of defeat, and thousands of construction workers, who had been engaged on the erection of defences against the anticipated invasion of the Continent by the Allies, were transferred to the building of launching areas for the new weapons.

In the meantime attacks on the *No-Ball* sites, in the first few months of 1944, continued with some success and a further reconnaissance over Picardy, Normandy and Artois indicated that work on the majority had been abandoned. Those that did show signs of activity received more visits from the RAF but the War Office believed that a much simplified system of launching the pilotless aircraft was under construction.

This was the case. Flakregiment 155(W), now almost mobile, was building "modified sites" of minimal construction with a ramp, concrete roads and a few essential buildings. Each site took about six days to erect and could be abandoned when discovered by the Allied bombers.

The Germans were certainly not cricket enthusiasts but many of the officers in High Command knew of a word straight from cricket anthology, No-Ball. By January, 1944, the codename for the Allied bombing of the flying bomb sites was hardly a secret but to confuse the enemy two new words were introduced — Diver for flying bombs and Big Ben for rockets.

Defence of London

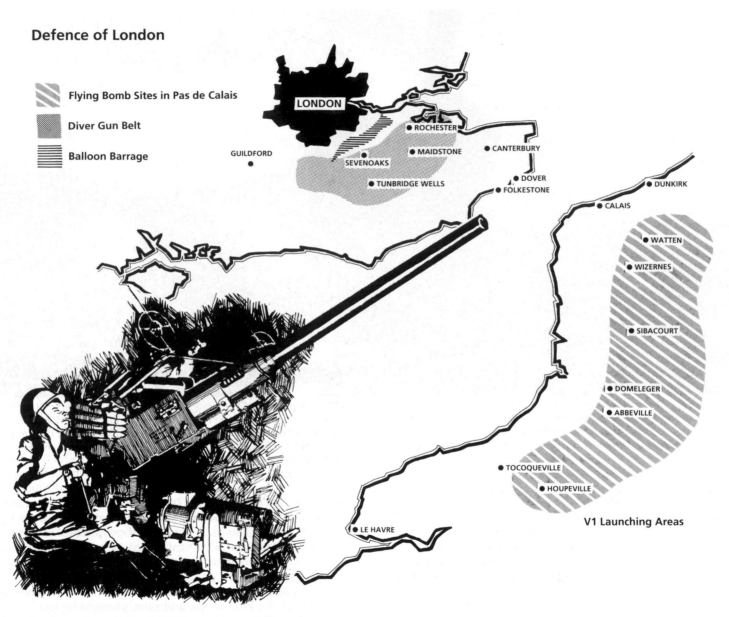

Flying Bomb Sites in Pas de Calais

Diver Gun Belt

Balloon Barrage

LONDON

GUILDFORD

● ROCHESTER

● MAIDSTONE

● CANTERBURY

● SEVENOAKS

● TUNBRIDGE WELLS

● DOVER

● FOLKESTONE

● DUNKIRK

● CALAIS

● WATTEN

● WIZERNES

● SIBACOURT

● DOMELEGER

● ABBEVILLE

● TOCOQUEVILLE

● HOUPEVILLE

V1 Launching Areas

● LE HAVRE

This drawing shows the anti-Diver defence measures. Fighters were the first line of defence, patrolling the Channel and the Kent and Sussex coast. They were backed by a concentrated belt of guns in front of a balloon barrage that grew thicker as the campaign progressed. The shaded area in France shows the V1 launching areas.

Falling like flies

AFTER many delays and frustrations caused by the Allied advance through Normandy, the Luftwaffe units responsible for launching the next wave of flying bombs finally got their act together and, in the 24 hours from midday on Thursday June 15, more than 200 missiles were fired. Several crashed directly after launch, killing 10 French civilians, but more than 60 got through to London.

The men on the anti-aircraft batteries in Kent and Greater London could hardly believe their luck as wave after wave of enticing targets came rattling over, all flying a straight course and all trailing a flaring exhaust. The gunners greeted the monsters with more enthusiasm than accuracy and aimed wildly into the air, cheering madly when the sudden cut-out by the engine seemed to indicate yet another score. "Look", shouted one man, "they are shooting the bastards down like flies."

It did not take long for the people of Kent and the men on the surburban batteries to realise that they were now under attack from the first of Hitler's "secret weapons". Mrs Greta Flanders of Tunbridge Wells was 13 years old when she heard her father say to her mother: "Quick Ada, get the children up and come and see this lot. The bloody Huns are sending over planes on fire."

"We looked out from a back bedroom window across the valley from Forest Road over to Pembury. In the dark night sky the bright sinister lights shone out over the heavens. I remember the noise, the dreaded drone of the engine like nothing I had heard before. Three or four flew low over Tunbridge Wells and faded away into the distance. We shuddered and clung together as yet more of the horrors flared their way up from the coast. Come the morning — in the grey dawn the world looked forbidding as I walked to the bus stop to go to school. The planes were still coming over, the droning thud, thud of the engines was so frightening. I just felt sick and frozen with fear. The regulars waited for the bus into town, everyone chattering about Hitler's new secret weapon. I remember thinking, why aren't they all scared like me, but then looking back it was like the Battle of Britain all over again."

33

By the end of June the deployment had swollen to 376 heavy guns and 576 light guns On the South Coast the RAF Regiment manned 560 light anti-aircraft weapons. Photograph shows a Mount machine gun, twin Cal. .50inch, M.33inch. The weapons mounted are .50 Browning M2HB models. The people watching this demonstration are local dignitaries from Hythe.

General Pile's Mattress

WHEN the flying bombs were first identified, General Pile, Commander-in-Chief of Anti-Aircraft Command had a mammoth task. His plan, prepared weeks earlier, was to instal 400 heavy anti-aircraft guns on the seaward side of the North Downs, stretching from East Grinstead, across Kent to Gravesend in a belt about five miles deep, with searchlights to assist the fighters at night. At first AA.Command acted cautiously to the attack but when the bombs started coming over in big salvoes, General Pile knew he had to work quickly.

He thought it would take him about 18 days to redeploy his defences — an estimate that had not gone unchallenged. Commanders of five American A.A. battalions placed at his disposal boasted that they would manage it in four days. They were wrong. The first guns were installed in their new locations in less than 24 hours in a military manoeuvre that was an outstanding success.

Experience had shown that the mobile 3.7 inch gun which had to be traversed by hand was "no match for the flying bomb". On Monday June 19, General Pile decided that all AA Command mobile 3.7 inch guns should be replaced by the static, power-controlled equipment. Instead of constructing a solid concrete base for the guns, which would have taken many months, the command's engineers devised the "Pile Mattress" — a movable lattice-work of steel rails and sleepers, filled with ballast.

Static guns were uprooted from all parts of England and sent south. More than 700 "Pile mattresses" were eventually made, requiring 35 miles of railway lines and 22,500 sleepers.

ATS girls — a spotter and height-finder operator — look on with some apprehension as an AA gunner points to the characteristic shape of a flying bomb rattling towards their gun-site command post. Their next duty was to call the operations room with exact information on the direction from which the plotter would calculate the possible height. Reports followed from other Observer Posts and the position of the bomb was traced on the main table, with the information being related to Fighter Control. If the noise of the motor suddenly stopped an observer would give his call-sign over the field telephone and add "Diver-cut". The plotter at the table would shout the information across the operations room, adding the identification number "Diver 167-cut". A crash counter was placed beside the last reported position of the missile. Somewhere outside there would be an explosion and a plume of smoke.

The Daily Telegraph 4 A.M.

and Morning Post

No. 27,775   LONDON, WEDNESDAY, JUNE 21, 1944   Printed in LONDON and MANCHESTER   PRICE 1½d.

ALLIES 3½ MILES FROM CHERBOURG

NAZIS REPORT LAND, SEA, AIR ATTACK

FLEET CUTS OFF ALL ESCAPE BY SEA

BRITISH HOLD PANZERS EAST OF TILLY

Advanced American patrols were reported last night to have infiltrated through the outer defences of Cherbourg and reached to within 3½ miles of the great port.

The main forces are believed to be four to five miles away, which would mean they had broken into the first of the three defensive zones in an advance of 15 miles in 24 hours.

This news came soon after Rennes radio had announced an all-out attack by land, sea and air against the fortress, which, it stated, Rundstedt had ordered must be defended to the last man.

The radio, quoting "last-minute reports," declared that Allied heavy naval guns shelled Cherbourg throughout yesterday, while four-engined bombers pounded the fortifications.

Despatches from correspondents with Americans closing in on an 18-mile front from the south and south-east stated that a battle for a height overlooking the port had begun.

PILOTLESS PLANE SHOT-DOWN OVER ENGLAND BY R.A F. FIGHTERS

One of the pilotless planes, which has been shot down by R.A.F. fighter aircraft over Southern England, lying with its tail in the foreground. Fighter pilots from a neighbouring airfield examine the wreckage to discover, if possible, more about its vulnerability.

TILLY TAKEN AFTER SEE-SAW BATTLE

NAZIS LEAVE TOWN A WRECK

From CHRISTOPHER BUCKLEY,
Daily Telegraph Special Correspondent
WITH THE BRITISH FORCES IN
NORMANDY,
Tuesday Morning.

Tilly is ours. This little village, which cost us 10 days of repeated fighting, has been the scene of a see-saw struggle grimly reminiscent of the last war.

Again and again it has seemed nearly cleared; again and again German infantry units and minor have infiltrated back into

---

WOMEN WATCH BATTLE FOR CHERBOURG

ALLIED GUNS CHEERED

From RICHARD McMILLAN

BEFORE CHERBOURG, Tuesday.
Chasing the last three remnants of two German divisions into Cherbourg, the Americans have begun the last battle for the port at its gates.

The attack opened at 5 p.m. to-day. Our artillery barrage began its shattering blows to break what may be the last line guarding the port.

I watched thousands of United States infantrymen trudging down the highways or cutting through the country lanes towards the battle line.

Many bridges which should have

RUSSIANS TAKE VIIPURI: BREAK 2 DEFENCE RINGS

1940 FRONTIER REACHED

The Russians have captured Viipuri, the fortress and port at the northern end of the Karelian Isthmus and the southern gateway to Finland.

This important success—gained 10 days after the opening of the Soviet offensive in the Karelian Isthmus, in which three defence zones were reduced—was announced last night by Marshal Stalin in an Order of the Day addressed to Gen.

SAW ROBOT RUNWAY DESTROYED BY BOMBS

FIRST EYE-WITNESS ACCOUNT OF PAS DE CALAIS RAID

From CORNELIUS RYAN
Daily Telegraph Special Correspondent
AT A U.S. 9TH AIR FORCE MARAUDER BASE,
Tuesday.

This evening I looked down on one of Hitler's pilotless plane launching platforms in the Pas de Calais area and saw bombs from this group march right across it.

The target was so cunningly hidden that the formation made no less than four bombing runs before it was definitely located and destroyed.

It lay at the intersection of a cross-roads and the actual launching platform was practically invisible from the air because it ran along the road, its white concrete structure merging with the colour of the roadway.

FEWER ROBOTS GET ACROSS CHANNEL

By Our Air Correspondent
Fewer of the pilotless planes reached Southern England yesterday than on previous days of the Nazi "meteor" bombing. Two main reasons for this seem to be:

1.—Hour-by-hour plastering of the runways in the Pas de Calais region of Northern France from which the robots are launched [details P6];

2.—The gale which raged over the Straits from a north-easterly direction, reaching at times a force of 60 m.p.h.

Many hundreds of tons of bombs rained down on the robot bases, for the first time defined as situated between Calais and Abbeville. Although cunningly camouflaged in densely wooded areas, the installations were identified and repeatedly hit in the most devastating assault yet made on these targets. [Picture, P5.]

All types of Allied aircraft were

Through binoculars the platform appeared to be a long, shallow affair, about 200ft long and 25ft wide, rising steeply at one end, and just behind it stood a small, square concrete building—apparently the control point.

From our height it was just a mere pinpoint, and on measuring it I found it to be about the length of the point of my pencil—about one sixteenth of an inch.

At the briefing, the importance of destroying the target was impressed upon the pilots and crews. Three senior officers of this group personally led squadrons in the formation. They were Lt.-Col. C. W. Lockhart, Lt.-Col. D. L. Weiss, and Lt.-Col. H. G. Hankey, with whom flew the Air Executive Officer at this station, Lt.-Col. Sherman Beaty.

We crossed the French coast at 12,000ft and began the "hunt" for the launching platform.

I could see the terrific effects of the large-scale bombing by Fortresses, Liberators and the R.A.F. in the past few days. All over the area the ground was pitted with bomb

---

"AMERICAN troops are on the Cherbourg peninsula and the US Ninth Air Force Marauders are dropping their bombs on the 'robot runways' near Calais." British people, reading this news on Wednesday June 21, 1944, had every reason to believe that the sites would soon be obliterated or overrun, and the flying bomb campaign would fizzle out before it had really started.

In fact a few sites were captured by the Americans, advancing towards Cherbourg. These were situated in the Cotentin peninsula and aligned on Plymouth or Bristol but the Germans were still building their modified sites, and it was from these that the V1 bombardment was coming. For the bomber crews it was not too difficult to find the sites, thanks to photographic intelligence, but to destroy them was another matter, despite the enthusiasm of the Daily Telegraph reporter.

By June 18, about 70 modified sites had been located and thousands of bombs dropped in heavy daylight raids. By mid-July more than 3,000 sorties were flown but, according to Colonel Wachtel's war diary, only four sites were silenced and about 38 badly damaged. In fact he was never short of bombs to fire, or ramps to fire them on; his problem was that trains, trucks, roads and railway lines were being destroyed, hampering the transportation of missiles to the sites.

Tempests of Newchurch

LIKE the bombers in France, the fighters in Kent and Sussex were not having things all their own way. The Spitfire, the Mustang and the Thunderbolts were experiencing some difficulty in matching the speed of the flying bombs and it was discovered that the Tempest V, which could reach speeds of 416 mph at low level, was the only aircraft capable of consistently intercepting and overtaking its robot prey. In view of this No 3 Tempest Squadron, one of three which formed 150 Wing, found itself in the front line of "Diver" missions and, from Newchurch on Romney Marsh, led the battle in the sky against the flying bomb.

Wing Commander Roland Beamont, commanding 150 Wing, with Sergeant Bob Cole of No 3 Squadron as his No 2 went into action just after dawn on June 16 and overtook his first V1 over Folkestone. It was flying at 370 mph. In his book *My Part of The Sky*, Beamont writes: "I missed completely with my first burst. Another short burst hit its port outer wing; and then with all the remaining ammunition a long burst hit it first on the fuselage, without immediate effect, and finally on the engine which stopped and it began to go down. The V1 slowed rapidly but remained on an even keel and, as I overtook it on the port side, I was able to get a quick look at its slim, pointed fuselage, high-mounted ram-jet engine at the back, and short stubby wings. It was painted dull grey overall and the jet pipe at the back was smoke-blacked. I called in Bob Cole to finish it off, which he did with a well-aimed burst and it rolled over on its back and dived into a field south of Maidstone, exploding with a lot of flame and black smoke".

On that first day, reports were coming in of more successes and by nightfall 150 Wing had shot down eight flying bombs. Back at Newchurch, Beamont and Cole learnt that their V1 was not the first to be shot down by a fighter; they had been beaten to it by one hour by a Mosquito night fighter flown by Flight Lieutenant Musgrave.

Beamont and his Wing learned a lot in those first few hours about the flying bomb and how to destroy it. They found that opening fire at 200 yards was the best range for effectiveness but there was great danger in exploding the warhead. This was duly confirmed the next day when a V1 was exploded by cannon fire and the aircraft went straight through the fireball, returning safely but streaked with smoke. The pilot was burned on the forearm.

Wing Commander Roly Beamont, who commanded the 150 Newchurch Wing was the pilot responsible for developing the tactics to be used against the V1. He recommended to Fighter Command that only the Tempest, Spitfire X1V and boosted Mustang should be involved in Diver operations and that the freelancing Thunderbolts and all other units should be banned from the main attack area between Dover and Eastbourne. He also suggested that the Observer Corps should be deployed round the coastline armed with distress rockets which could be fired in any required direction. This would enable the fighter pilot —already under radar control — to see the point of convergence of the rockets as an indication to where the missile might be. The recommendations were accepted and Beamont and his Tempest marksmen went on to become Britain's first well-known fly-bomb aces.

The pilot who tipped the balance

WEST Malling, on the doodlebug path to London, was another airfield earmarked for anti-diver operations and when the night-fighters moved out in mid-June they left 91 and 96 Squadrons as the squadrons in residence to combat the new onslaught and uphold the traditions of this famous fighter station.

The two squadrons swung vigorously into action, their pilots bagging a number of V1's, but it was 91 Squadron, flying the new Spitfire XIV, now fitted with the powerful Griffon engine, who became West Malling's best-known doodlebug destroyers. On Friday June 23, one of their ace pilots, a tall Australian, Flying Officer Ken Collier, discovered a method of V1 destruction which is now part of aviation folklore.

On that Friday evening, Collier and his colleagues were scrambled at 9.50 pm to intercept Divers approaching from the Channel. Collier sighted his quarry from a few miles distance. It was flying on its steady course at 2,500 feet so Collier dived down to intercept, closed in and pressed the trigger. The burst was accurate but it had no effect. The bomb continued to spit fire, so Collier closed in and fired again. He was out of ammunition.

Flying at 330 mph, he glanced down to find a place without any buildings around, overtook the missile and flew alongside it. With the tip of his wing, Collier attempted to throw the doodlebug on its back. It failed so he tried again and with great satisfaction watched it spin down, crash in a field and explode.

The Australian pilot, delighted with his success, reported to the intelligence officer when he landed but his story was greeted with considerable scepticism. His colleagues, seasoned pilots, could not quite believe that anyone could have the audacity to fly alongside 120 kg of dynamite, moving at 330 miles an hour and perform a "circus trick". A shout from the mechanics ended all their doubts; they had discovered fresh black paint on the wing tip of Collier's Spitfire. It was, of course, the signal for a party in the mess.

The following week the story of Collier's daring act appeared in the Kent Messenger. "Quick thinking and cool courage on the part of a fighter pilot probably saved serious casualties from a flying bomb in Southern England on Friday evening......the pursuing pilot manoeuvered his plane close to it and diverted it from its course by tipping the wing. As a result the bomb dropped in some gardens at the rear of an old people's home."

The name of the Squadron was not given, nor the name of the pilot but it became the most talked about technique and soon many

Flying Officer Ken Collier (right), the Australian who tipped the balance, with Jean Maridor.

airmen were employing the same method. Sadly, up until now, Collier's feat has never been officially recognised, for he was shot down and killed in December 1944 and had little time to reflect on his "doodlebug days". Then, after the war, 91 Squadron's record book went missing, coming to light only recently after many exhaustive searches. The book is now in the hands of Peter Hall, the Squadron's historian, who made the historic rediscovery.

The official RAF history states that the first time a flying bomb was toppled over to fall prematurely out of control took place on June 23 by a Spitfire pilot. All enquiries in squadron records to find the pilot drew a blank.

A Tempest V of the 150 Wing from Newchurch chases a flying bomb at low level over Kent. The black and white stripes of the Tempest, introduced for easy identification during the invasion period, can be seen. Wing Commander Beamont had the guns on his Tempests altered to converge at 300 yards. This increased the effect of the firepower against the V1 and No 3 Squadron became the top-scoring doodlebug Squadron with more than 300 kills.

Frenchman was a hero of Kent

Jean and Jean pictured on the July day she introduced him to her parents. It was the only time they were to meet him.

A photograph of Jean Holme in 1992, living at the time with her husband in Sevenoaks.

ANOTHER pilot of 91 Squadron with a particular anger towards the doodlebug and the way it indiscriminately killed civilians was the Frenchman, Capitain Jean Maridor. In April, 1944 he joined the West Malling wing under Wing Commander Bobby Oxspring and, with his colleagues, lived in a tent on the airfield.

On his arrival at West Malling, Maridor met and fell in love with a pretty WAAF, Section Officer Jean Lambourn. The couple, in the tradition of the pace of life which existed at the time, planned a wedding in August at Oxford where Mr and Mrs Lambourne lived. Jean Maridor's life was hectic. In the few months he was at West Malling, the handsome Frenchman courted his bride-to-be, helped with the arrangements for the wedding and shot down doodlebugs in numerous day-time patrols of mid-Kent.

Maridor knew his zone well. He had flown on many operational sorties in the south-east and on the other side of the Channel and had recently been involved in fighter sweeps and shipping reconnaissance operations. On one occasion he was returning alone from such a mission when he spotted a number of Focke Wulfes that were on a bombing mission to Folkestone. Summoning help from other members of his squadron he went into the attack and spectators below cheered as they watched the harassed Germans drop their bombs in the sea and flee back to the Continent. Maridor was a superb pilot and his almost fanatical hatred of the pilotless projectile was a feature of many late-night conversations in the Mess at West Malling.

Towards the end of July, at the height of the campaign, 91 Squadron was transferred to Deanland, near Lewes, where they continued with their anti-Diver duties, hoping that Saturday August 10 — the day of Jean's wedding to Jean — would be sufficiently free of robots to allow some of them to attend the service.

There was to be no service. On August 3, one week before the big day, Jean Maridor attacked his last flying bomb. Chasing the missile from the direction of Rolvenden, he pressed the trigger and hit the bomb but it had no effect. Maridor knew the danger of getting too near to his prey, but it was not in his nature to allow it to escape so he closed in again. Realising he was rather too close to some buildings below he held fire but, as a result, moved even nearer to the missile. He fired, the warhead exploded, but a wing was blown off the Spitfire and the two crashed into the Kentish countryside near Benenden. A number of cottages close to Walkhurst Farm were damaged by the blast. Jean Maridor was killed. He was 23.

Medway House,
Benenden,
Kent.

11. 11. 44.

Dear Mr Lambourn,

I wish I could tell you more about the terrible accident to Captain Maridor. As you can imagine it all happened so quickly we had no time to see much.

We were told here that in trying to save the hospital and the school where we live he shot at the flying bomb rather too close. The plane was cut in half and flew over the school.

Will you tell your daughter from us all here that his gallant deed saved the lives of soldiers in Hospital and many small children. I feel this is not much help to you all but it is all I can tell you. I am sending you one of the shells that we picked up in the grounds, it may be a little comfort to your daughter to have one of the shells shot from Capt. Maridor's plane.

Yours sincerely

(signed) Barbara Sharp

His funeral was held at Brookwood, Surrey attended by many mourners, including General Valin, head of the Free French Air Force. Of the many wreaths, his fiancée, who later married and became Jean Holme, remembers one in particular. It came from the town clerk of Folkestone and contained a simple message which read: "To Jean Maridor, with grateful thanks from the people of Folkestone".

Flight Lieutenant J.C.Musgrave, of South Lincs and Flight Sergeant F.W.Somwell, Observer of Leeds who were flying a No. 605 Squadron Mosquito over the Channel, in the early hours of Friday June 16, when they encountered a "pilotless plane" coming from the Continent. The Mosquito turned, pursued it and opened fire. It exploded with a tremendous flash and dived into the sea giving Flight Lt. Musgrave the distinction of being the first RAF pilot to shoot down a V1.

The Aldwych massacre

The scene of the Aldwych massacre soon after the bomb had fallen. There were two explosions in the West End on this day. The first, just after midday, hit the roof of the annexe to the Regent Palace Hotel in Brewer Street, killing a chambermaid.

THE office girls were sunbathing on the roof of the Air Ministry building, Adastral House, in the Aldwych and the street below was crowded with lunchtime shoppers. It was a glorious midsummer day and, above the chatter of the people and the noise of London's traffic, few heard the approach of a flying bomb. High above The Strand the engine cut out and the missile glided down silently. It struck the road 40 feet in front of Adastral House and turned a peaceful summer scene into one of dreadful carnage. Forty eight people were killed on this Friday lunchtime. Casualties amounted to more than 200.

One of the injured was Miss Cecille Daly who worked for the Foreign Office in Ingersoll House, opposite the Air Ministry and next door to Bush House, home of the BBC External Services. Part of her job was top secret — to prepare leaflets for dropping over France and Belgium and propaganda speeches to answer the words of William Joyce (Lord Haw Haw). On Friday June 30 she reported for duty early after lunch. It was 1.50pm.

"I like fresh air and, as it was a sunny day, I opened my office window, when suddenly there was a terrible explosion. The bomb impacted on a row of buses and, when the dust lifted, there was a scene of terrible slaughter — pavements were littered with the dead and wounded and, on the road were the twisted, unrecognisable frames of a line of buses. The sunbathing girls had been blown to eternity. My secret papers had been scattered far and wide and I was lucky to be suffering only cuts and bruises. The blast damaged the face of Bush House and the two statues over the door had their arms blown off. I was taken to hospital in one of the many ambulances which arrived and, on the way, the ambulance crew asked me to help give injections to the badly wounded. After being bandaged up I went to see my mother, herself an ambulance driver, and my father, a Civil Defence warden, to tell them that I was OK."

The Aldwych injured are carried away on stretchers.

THE borough of Croydon received its first flying bomb on the night of Thursday June 15, when one fell at the junction of Avenue and Warminster Roads. On that night several people were killed or injured. But this was only the forerunner of a bombardment which was to last, unbroken, for nearly three months. Croydon, it seemed, had been singled out for the special attention of robot aircraft.

There was scarcely a road in the town which escaped damage and during one exceptional weekend as many as 15 flying bombs crashed in residential areas. The record number to fall in one night was eight. This was a night of grief and terror with hundreds made homeless. Thousands of properties were damaged and the emergency services were strained to the limit.

In the first full week of the attack, 22 flying bombs landed in the borough, which included Norwood and Thornton Heath. There were 24 in the second week and 27 in the third. By the end of the campaign 142 missiles had landed in Croydon's streets. It was the V1's greatest battlefield.

Few people in Croydon enjoyed a full night's sleep during the flying bomb campaign. They took it in snatches and declined to go into the shelters when an attack was imminent. It was safer to listen for the familiar spluttering noise, wait for the jet engine to "shut off", gauge its possible target and then look around for any convenient cover from the blast. The "cut-out" was the danger signal that Croydon came to know all too well; for this meant that a home, school, factory, shop, church or hospital would almost certainly be hit. Few fell in open ground. Those that continued on their lethal, predetermined course were destined to create the same chaos and heartbreak in Streatham, Mitcham, Wandsworth, Penge and Sydenham.

In all, 58,968 houses in Croydon were damaged — more than the total number of houses in the town, explained by the fact that many homes sustained further damage after being repaired.

To help carry out repairs, 1,500 workers were brought in from other parts of the country and accommodated in schools, halls and temporary huts. A party of men from Scotland and Ireland arrived and were billeted in huts in Aurelia Road, West Croydon. A few hours later a V1 crashed on top of the huts and 11 of the newcomers were killed.

Courageous Croydon

(142 flying bombs)

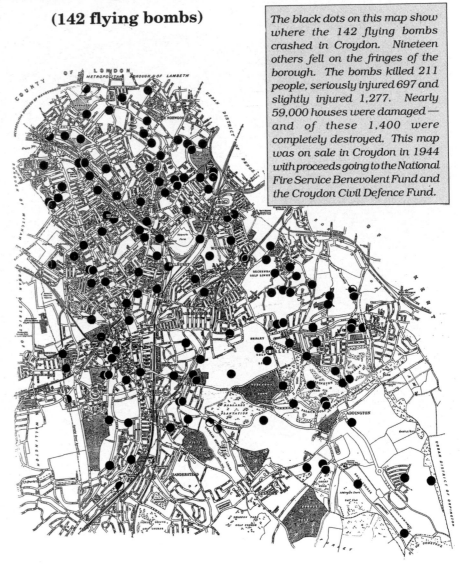

The black dots on this map show where the 142 flying bombs crashed in Croydon. Nineteen others fell on the fringes of the borough. The bombs killed 211 people, seriously injured 697 and slightly injured 1,277. Nearly 59,000 houses were damaged — and of these 1,400 were completely destroyed. This map was on sale in Croydon in 1944 with proceeds going to the National Fire Service Benevolent Fund and the Croydon Civil Defence Fund.

This is Moffatt Road, Thornton Heath where 14 people died on the evening of July 4. Mrs A.E.Adams, a resident of Moffatt Road told the Croydon Advertiser: "It was 9 pm and my mother and I had just switched on the wireless when we heard it coming over. It was so low it seemed on the roof itself. I managed to pull the plug from the wall so the wireless was off and we just had time to get behind the dining room door in the corner of the room. The noise I shall never forget. It was the roof being blown off and the front of the house took the worst of the blast. The next thing we knew was a kind ARP Warden telling us to leave immediately and take our valuables with us." Photograph shows the scene in Moffatt Road the next day.

Dejection and defiance in the "bravest town of all"

WHEN the censor allowed the Croydon Times to publish this photograph the caption read: *"Pictures of dejected refugees driven from bombed German towns by the advance of the Allies were often published in 1944 but they did not exceed the misery and pathos of the story told by this photograph. Whatever the German families had to suffer was only retribution for the kind of thing which became an everyday scene during the fly-bomb attacks."*

During this period life went on in Croydon very much as usual. Thousands, of course, had been evacuated but those who remained maintained a tremendous calmness in the face of such adversity. The women in their homes went on with their housework — and their part-time jobs in the factories. When windows were smashed and ceilings brought down they just patched everything up as best they could.

Cinemas in the town remained open, with the exception of two that were closed for repairs. Trams and buses did not stop unless the driver happened to see a bomb approaching. Then the bus would stop and there would be a scramble for the floor.

Ten people died when a newsagent's shop opposite The Windsor Castle pub in Brighton Road, South Croydon was hit on July 18. Those killed were either walking along the street on their way to work, or calling in the shop for their morning papers.

Tea is served to repair workers from a YMCA canteen outside the bomb-wrecked Mission Hall at Old Town, Croydon. The bomb fell onto Cranmer Road during the night of July 26-27.

Worst week of the campaign

THE first week of July saw the flying bomb attack reach its zenith. In seven days more than 800 missiles were launched and, although many got through to cause death and destruction in London, the county of Kent suffered badly from those which either stalled and fell, or were shot down by the guns or fighters.

The popular term for a bomb crashing in Kent was "open country". But "open country" as Alderman E.S.Oak-Rhind, chairman of Kent's Civil Defence Committee, pointed out at the time, was dotted with villages, cottages, farms and houses with, here and there, a big town. "A flying bomb exploding in the air, let alone on the ground, will strip the roofs, bring down the ceilings, shatter the windows of all beneath. A flying bomb will often take somebody's life — in order to save London."

The worst day of all was Sunday July 2 when 161 VI's crossed the coast. They were attacked by the Spitfires and Tempests of the RAF. They were hindered by a vast, concentrated belt of guns and they faced a balloon barrage that had been growing thicker by the day. Scores came down in Kent but many got through to their target.

During the week that followed, flying bombs were shot down on Folkestone, East Peckham, Maidstone, Ruckinge and Higham. A total of seven people were killed and 68 injured.

This V1 fell into an orchard at Bobbing, near Sittingbourne. No-one was hurt. Trevor Horton, now of Folkestone, remembers two Spitfires chasing this flying bomb and one of them tipping it over. It exploded in the orchard and he found hundreds of unripe apples lying on the ground.

This was "open country"

The village centre at Pluckley, near Ashford, the Horseshoe Inn at East Farleigh, near Maidstone, an oast house (normally used for drying hops) at Tudeley, near Tonbridge — all visited by doodlebugs in the summer of 1944. This, according to the War Ministry, was open country.

In the early hours of July 2, a flying bomb fell in Albemarle Road, Beckenham near the junction with the High Street. Three died, 30 were injured and 11 shops were destroyed. The incident happened in the early hours of the morning. Civil Defence personnel and rescue equipment were soon on the scene and, before it was light, an emergency food van was handing out refreshments to both the homeless and the rescuers.

It was quite uncanny how the flying bombs were landing on or near military targets. The Air Ministry building in the Aldwych, the Guards Barracks at Wellington Square and the Newlands Military Camp at Charing in Kent were three such sites. The worst of all came at breakfast time on Monday July 3 when the US Army billets at Sloane Court, Chelsea received a direct hit, killing 64 soldiers and 10 civilians.

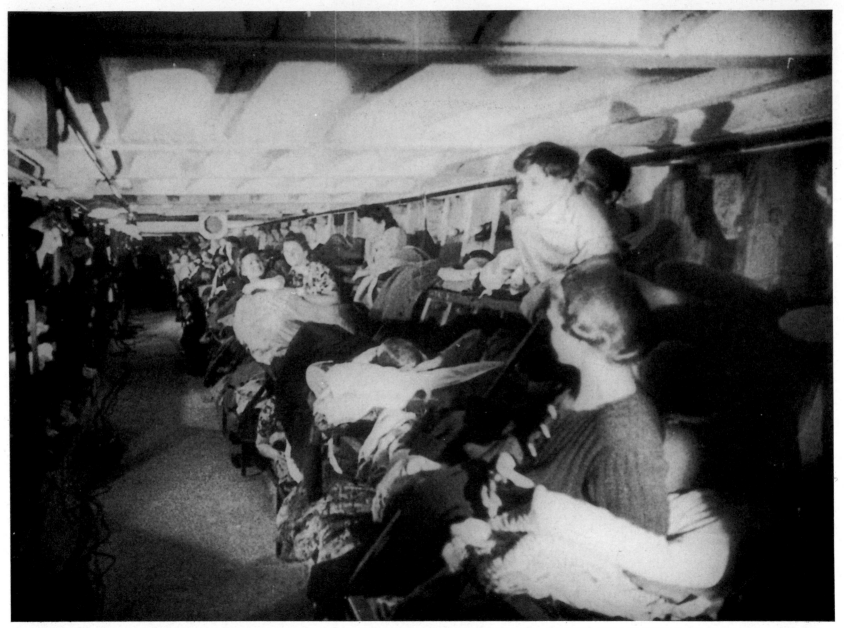

By early July there was a rapid increase in the number of people sleeping in the London Underground — the numbers were estimated to be in excess of 70,000.

Raid on the caves

IN France, Bomber Command hammered away night after night at the launch sites and what were thought to be the supply depots but it had little effect on the frequency of the attacks on London and the south-east. Dr Jones began to think that the bombs were being distributed from other sites, so he set his agents to work. Back came the answer; there were three underground fly-bomb storage depots. The largest of these was at St Leu d'Esserent, in caves in the Oise valley, just north of Paris. The second was at Nucourt, north-west of Paris and the third at Rilly-la-Montagne, south of Rheims, in a railway tunnel.

Dr Jones recommended that the storage sites be attacked and, in the last week of June, the Eighth Army Air Force dropped so many bombs that two of the three were obliterated. At Nucourt, 241 V1's were buried beyond recovery by the collapse of the roof of the caves and at Rilly, the cavern entrance collapsed rendering it useless.

St Leu, however, was less vulnerable, owing to the greater thickness of the limestone roof. For the Germans it was the perfect home for their flying bomb supply and they had adapted the caves with great efficiency, building railway tracks, living quarters, canteens with water and electricity supplies. There were hundreds of men employed in the building work and, among these, were members of the French Resistance who sent back detailed plans of the storage galleries. It appeared that as many as 37 train loads of flying bombs were entering the caves on a single day and thousands of missiles were stored there. Orders were given to attack the sites again.

Heavier bombs were needed for St Leu and Dr Jones recommended "Tallboy", the big streamlined bomb developed by Barnes Wallis, which had already ruptured the Ruhr Dams. On the night of July 4 — 5, 1944, Wing Commander Leonard Cheshire, led his famous 617 Squadron on a raid of the caves at St Leu d'Esserent. The 12,000 pound

This was the entrance to one of Germany's secret flying bomb factories. The rail track led directly to the caves, which were almost two miles underground. The site was heavily bombed by the Allied Air Force and the photograph, taken later in the campaign, shows American soldiers on guard at the entrance.

bombs were dropped. They blocked the main tunnel and several others collapsed. The approach road was rendered impassable. The railway, the branch tracks, the blockhouses and the gantries were blown to pieces. It was an awesome demonstration of air power which had an immediate effect, for the average number of flying bombs launched against London dropped, from 100 a day, to fewer than 70.

According to Dr Jones, the reduction in the rate of the bombardment meant the defences were less saturated and the gunners and fighters were able to achieve a higher rate of success. Before the attack on the caves, 40 per cent of the bombs entering the defences were being shot down. This rose to well over 50 per cent after St Leu had been bombed. "The original Wachtel plan", said Dr Jones, "had been to fire the bombs in salvoes, so that while one was being engaged several others would get through."

Fortunately Colonel Wachtel never achieved the necessary synchronisation.

The destruction caused by the flying bomb which fell at Hollington, Hastings on Friday afternoon, July 16. Pursued by fighters, the robot was hit and dived among small houses in Old Church Road and Hollington Old Lane. Three people lost their lives and 47 were injured. Many were rendered homeless and accommodated at the Castleham rest centre.

Above: When a doodlebug fell at Westfield in July, an inventive resident placed a union jack next to the remains of the bomb, which was lodged in a hedge, and a notice inviting passers-by to make a donation. A substantial amount was collected and donated to the Red Cross.

Left: One of the worst incidents in Sussex occurred at Shortgate, Laughton on August 4 when a flying bomb fell on three cottages, which included a sub-post office, and completely demolished them. The postmistress, Mrs F.Tobitt and four others were killed. Picture shows the Bell Inn, on the opposite side of the road, which was also severely damaged.

"Well, that's one less for London"

ALONGSIDE the ARP wardens, the firemen and all those in the front line of rescue work during this hectic period of doodlebuggery, there was always a group of smiling, caring, hard working people quietly helping — members of the Women's Voluntary Service. They cooked, they washed-up, they gave comfort and they set up inquiry points at every incident. They acted as nurses, messengers and escorts. They ran mobile canteens where they dispensed hundreds of thousands of cups of tea. In the much-bombed borough of Beckenham alone, the WVS served 101,407 cups of tea, an average of 1,500 per flying bomb.

In Uckfield, the WVS Centre Organiser was Miss V.M.Porter who lived in Crowborough below three doodlebug lanes to London. More than 150 crashed in her area, many of them shot down by fighters, and her abiding memory today is the way that those people whose homes were destroyed frequently said — "well, that's one less for London".

On one occasion Miss Porter saw a Spitfire chasing a Vl. The pilot waited until he was past the village of Wadhurst, then opened fire. The shots hit the giro mechanism, the doodlebug turned full circle and dived onto Green Square, Wadhurst. Miss Porter remembers when the children of Uckfield were evacuated. She was standing with them on Uckfield station when they saw a Vl overhead and then suddenly the engine stopped. There was pandemonium but all was well. The missile glided on before crashing in open countryside.

WVS members have many memorable stories. One concerns a toothless old man who was sitting outside a bombed house in West Ewell. They gave him a cup of tea, and offered him a bun, which he refused. The old boy then returned to the debris of his home, scrabbled around for some time and then came back. "I'll have a bun, now", he said, "I've found my false teeth." On another occasion an elderly couple were rescued from under a table in a blitzed building. Arriving at the WVS incident point, the lady turned to her husband and said: "Now, dad, was it worth buying, or not ? I told you it was a bloody good table, didn't I".

When the alert sounded one day at Clapham, a man quickly grabbed his small children, popped them into the Anderson shelter and turned to look for his wife. Vl's were approaching and she was upstairs. He told her to hurry up and she yelled: "Wait a moment. I've got to find my dentures". "Listen you", came the reply. "They're dropping doodlebugs — not sandwiches."

Miss V.M.Porter, WVS Centre Organiser for Uckfield — a photograph taken in 1944.

Intertwined with humour there was always tragedy. One of the most tragic tasks for the WVS was tracing missing people and, on numerous occasions, breaking the news that a friend or relative was dead. The effect of blast from flying bombs was horrifying and on various occasions, men and women had all their clothes blown off. In his book *Women in Green, the story of the WVS*, Charles Graves writes that a policeman asked a member of the WVS if she could find a blanket for his colleague who, at that moment, was hiding behind a wall clad only in his boots. On another occasion, an elderly woman from Yorkshire was having a bath when the house collapsed. Six hours afterwards when the rescue squads were getting near her, she called out. "Ee, you'll get a surprise lads. I've nowt on."

One bomb, one fatality

THE toll of death, injury and damage to property from the flying bomb attacks was far greater than anyone had imagined and Londoners, in particular, wrote irate letters to their MP's demanding to have more details of the campaign and asking what the Government intended to do about it. As it was now impossible to apply the censorship policy any longer, Churchill agreed to make a statement in the House on July 6.

"Up to 6 am today 2,752 people have been killed by flying bombs and about 8,000 have been injured and detained in hospital. The number of flying bombs launched up to 6 am today was 2,754.

"The firing points in France have been continually attacked for several months and the total weight of bombs so far dropped on these and rocket targets in France and Germany, including Peenemunde, has now reached about 50,000 tons.

"The invisible battle has now crashed into the open. We shall now be able to watch its progress at fairly close quarters. Between 100 and 150 flying bombs, each weighing about one ton, are being discharged daily, and have been discharged for the last fortnight or so.

"Considering the modest weight and small penetrative power the damage done by blast effect has been extensive. It cannot be compared with the terrific destruction by fire and high explosive with which we have been assaulting Berlin, Hamburg, Cologne, and scores of other German cities and war manufacturing points...

"A very high proportion of the casualties have fallen upon London, which presents to the enemy a target 18 miles wide by 20 miles deep. It offers the unique target of the world for the use of a weapon of such inaccuracy. The flying bomb is a weapon literally and essentially indiscriminate in its nature, purpose and effect.

"The House will ask. What of the future? Is this attack going to get worse? Will the rocket-bomb come? Will more destructive explosions come? Will there be greater ranges ? I can give no guarantee that any of these evils will be finally prevented before the time comes when the soil from which these attacks come has been fully liberated.

"I must make it perfectly plain. I don't want any misunderstandings. We shall not allow the battle operations in Normandy, nor the attacks we are making against specific targets in Germany, to suffer. They come first. We must fit in our own domestic arrangements in the general scheme. There is no questioning of the slightest weakening of the battle. It may be a comfort to some that they are sharing in no small way the burdens of our soldiers overseas.

The Anderson shelter, which was like a small bicycle shed partly buried underground, really came into its own during the flying bomb campaign. It offered wonderful protection against falling masonry and blast as this photograph clearly shows. Two people emerge unharmed from their Anderson after a bomb had completely destroyed their home.

The brick surface shelters also saved many lives in the days of the doodlebug. Blast caused this street in Islington to collapse in a horrifyingly spectacular way but the surface shelters remained intact.. This type was most unpopular during the London air raids in 1940.

"London will never be conquered and we will never fail and that her renown, triumphing over every ordeal, will long shine among men."

Churchill told the House that he had visited various scenes of bomb explosions and spoken to a number of the injured of which there were now about 8,000 in hospital. He said that penicillin, which had only been available to the military, would now be given in the treatment of flying bomb casualties, It was a magnificent, robust Churchillian speech which cleared the air, answered a lot of questions and gave the chief censor a clearer picture of his future duties. Flying bombs were now officially landing in London!

CHAPTER 5: HEIGHT OF THE BATTLE

"The efficiency of my pupils is amazing. They have never failed to give a warning, and what is more they do not let it interfere with their lessons. The spotters on duty have a desk just outside the classroom door so they can hear the lesson, do their work and listen for the doodlebugs at the same time."

Miss Amy Barkley, headmistress, Otham School, near Maidstone

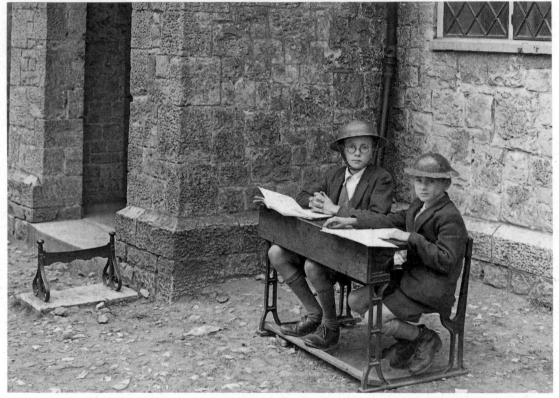

The people of "doodlebug alley" went about their everyday work with their eyes trained on the skies and their ears tuned in to that ghastly low-level roar. Offices, shops, factories and all public buildings posted "spotters" and at Otham Church of England primary school, the headmistress asked for volunteers to sit in the playground, wearing their tin hats and shout "doodlebug" whenever one approached. The class would then troop obediently into the shelter. This photograph, taken by the Kent Messenger in July, 1944, shows Gordon Spendly, aged 10 and Alan Chapman, eight, doing their spell of doodlebug spotting.

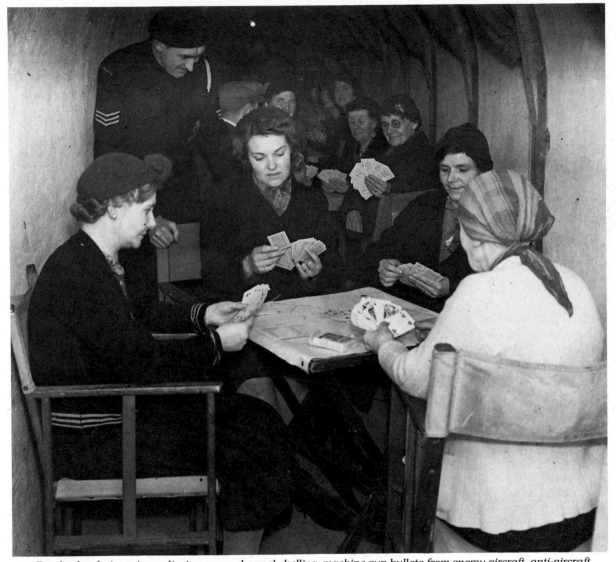

Bombs, landmines, incendiaries, cross channel shelling, machine gun bullets from enemy aircraft, anti-aircraft shells from "friendly" guns and now doodlebugs -- little wonder the people of Dover took to the shelters so often. This photograph shows some of the ladies of Kent's most-bombed town casually playing whist during a V1 alert. The tables were set out in one of the series of tunnels which runs under the White Cliffs. During the war, 199 civilians from Dover town were killed and 727 injured. More than 10,000 properties were damaged. Although many flying bombs came over only three crashed in the town and six flew slap bang into the cliffs between Folkestone and Dover. Hundreds came down on the beaches.

THE children of Otham became such proficient doodlebug spotters that other schools in Kent and Sussex adopted the same method, rather than trust the more official "alert" warning. At night, however, it was a different story. Thousands upon thousands of people lay in their beds listening for that tell-tale noise. They listened to the sound of the night fighters and they listened for the worst sound of all — silence. They knew then they had 15 seconds in which to find cover before an explosion could rip their home apart.

The people of London had their own spotters and alarm systems. At some factories a bell was rung and others had flashing red lights. At Ford's of Dagenham, there was a "six-pip" alert indicating imminent danger. Others just relied on their ears and then dived for the sturdiest desk.

There was a rapid increase in the number of people using the Underground — more than 70,000 by the middle of July. Some just slept there. Many Londoners, however, remained underground all day and went home just now and again to fetch food. There was a demand that the Government open up the deep shelters, which had been completed too late for the 1940-41 Blitz. The first to be opened was at Stockwell on Sunday July 9 when 4,000 people spent a happier night 130 feet below ground. A second shelter was opened four days later.

Photograph shows the guns being towed along the road over the marshes on their way to Rye in July 1944. It was between Rye Harbour and Camber that the biggest concentration of artillery in the country was established.

Goodbye Rye

SUSSEX'S first flying bomb fell in a field behind Mizbrooks Farm, Cuckfield at 4.20 am on Thursday June 13 — the second to land on British soil. Two days later, on Saturday June 15, anti-aircraft guns on the Sussex coast hit a second diver which crashed on the embankment of the Hastings railway line, the blast stripping tiles from the houses in nearby Bexhill Road. This was the prelude to a hectic two months in which East Sussex was rarely out of the action.

Altogether 775 doodlebugs were to fall in the county and many hundreds more fell in the sea around the coast. The AA gunbelt which stretched to Beachy Head was responsible for many of these "kills" and, as in Kent, they also caused considerable damage to property. In Portslade, Brighton, for example, 81 homes were hit by AA shells.

Sixteen flying bombs fell on Bexhill and although many properties were destroyed there were no civilian deaths. The first came down in Richmond Road in late June where it made a 30 foot crater in the middle of the road. It was in Bexhill that a missile, tracked all the

way from France, was seen heading straight for the town, flying exceptionally low. Two miles off the coast it turned westwards, passed over Beachy Head and then, inexplicably, turned again, flew south-east and crashed onto Boulogne from whence it came. Hastings and St Leonards received 14 doodlebugs, including one in Pevensey Road on June 23 which injured five people, one in Amherst Road on July 1 which caused two casualties and a third in Conqueror Road two days later in which there were 10 serious and 18 slight injuries.

Although only five missiles fell on Rye, the flying bomb period was the noisiest of the war for its inhabitants. The biggest concentration of artillery in the country, 1,300 gunners, was massed between Camber and Rye Harbour and the bulk of the population was moved to "safe quarters". The Grammar School was evacuated to Bedford and other children went to Blackpool and Monmouthshire. The rest were scattered throughout Cornwall, Somerset and Gloucestershire. Left in the town were the old people who refused to be driven out by Hitler, and those in business and factories of importance to the war effort.

Moving the guns

BY the beginning of July, the three groups of defenders — gunners, airmen and balloon crews — were so frequently getting in each other's way in their bid to shoot, tip or blast the VIs out of the sky that something had to be done, and quickly. Trigger-happy Americans and undisciplined AA batteries were blamed for illicit, freelance firing that destroyed not only flying bombs but RAF fighters. The Polish squadrons complained that the wings of their Mustangs were so perforated from "friendly fire" that they could be used as sieves and Roland Beamont, CO of the two squadrons of Tempests flying from Newchurch said his pilots spent much of their time trying to dodge the shell bursts of ack-ack.

Two Tempests were shot down by anti-aircraft guns in the first week of the battle but Wing Commander Beamont was able to retaliate in a rather bizarre fashion. A Tempest pilot shot down a flying bomb which crashed into the grounds of a country house used as a mess by the gunners. The explosion blew out all the windows in the mess as the gunners were having their breakfast. "No-one was hurt", said Beamont, "but the pilots came back from this particular sortie holding their sides."

Air Chief Marshal Hill, Commander-in-Chief of the Air Defence of Great Britain, himself flew on a number of sorties to assess the situation and decided that it was wrong to maintain the gun batteries inland; they should be redeployed to the coast. General Pile endorsed the plan and, on July 13, the greatest and most important decision in the battle against the flying bomb was made. The guns were to be moved to the coast, leaving the balloons where they were and creating two new areas for fighters alone, one between the balloons and the new gun belt and the other in front of the gun belt, over the sea.

Hundreds of guns and great reserves of ammunition were in position on the North Downs, thousands of miles of telephone cables had been laid and accommodation had been found for the gunners. "In short", said General Pile, "a small city was spread out between Redhill and the Thames and the proposal was that we should pick it up and transport it 30 or 40 miles south."

Only five days later another great military operation was completed. The guns were moved and resited between St Margaret's Bay and Cuckmere Haven. There were many batteries involved — 376 heavy and 572 light guns from General Pile's command, 16 90 mm guns from the US Army, 560 light guns manned by the RAF Regiment for

The New Defences July 1944

LEGEND
VI LAUNCHING AREAS
DIVER GUN BELT
BALLOON BARRAGE

airfield defence and 28 from the Royal Armoured Corps. The new "Diver" zone stretched 10,000 yards into the sea and 5,000 yards inland. The balloon barrage was increased, to 1,000 by July 21 and to 1,750 by the end of the month, and fighters had their own freedom of action between the guns and balloons and over the sea.

It was an enormous success. From their new position the gunners shot down 17 per cent of all flying bombs entering the gun belt in the first week. The score mounted from 24 per cent in the second week to 74 per cent in the last week of August. By then, those that escaped the fighters over the sea and the now-brilliant shooting of the gunners, met the fighters again inland. Hundreds of doodlebugs were again falling in "open countryside". As the weeks went by Kent was to suffer badly and so, to a lesser extent was Sussex but London, thanks to the co-operation that existed between the AA Command, Balloon Command and the RAF, could see, at last, a glimmer of hope on the horizon.

A 3.7 inch heavy battery takes up position at Sea Road, West Marina, St Leonards-on-Sea. Sussex in a move that turned out to be an extraordinary success. Of the new compact gun belt, General Pile said at the time that it would give the fighters plenty of room for interception over the Channel and plenty of room for interception behind the guns where they would be acting as wicket-keepers, with the balloons away in the distance as long stops. There was also more chance, he said, of bringing the flying bombs harmlessly down into the sea.

The "Brocks Benefit" over the skies of south Kent from one of the batteries of guns on Romney Marsh. Hundreds of gunners, both British and American, contributed to the barrage which brought down so many V1s. Now the great danger was not only from falling doodlebugs but shrapnel, for everything that went up had to come down.

Edna, Gladys, Molly and Marian of the 490 H.A.A Battery

The searchlight radar which helped Marian and her colleagues to improve the "kill" rate against the flying bomb.

Looking for love nests

AMONG the anti-aircraft batteries sent to the coast in mid-July was the 490th Heavy, which encamped at Lympne on the cliff above Romney Marsh in hurriedly erected tented accommodation. Like other batteries, there were plenty of women on the gun sites, including Marian (now Mills), a radar operator who recalls her days in the front line.

"On our arrival at Lympne, new American radar sets replaced our cumbersome Mark 2's and 3's, the cabins of which had to be rotated by hand in order to line up the aerial with the target. The American 584's had dish aerials rotating on a static cabin. It was much easier to get and stay on target even when the missile passed overhead. I can still feel the tension and thrill of those seconds when each operator called in turn — "on range", "on bearing", "on angle" and the No 1 called "on target" to the command post, the information being electrically passed to the gun positions. The speed of the flying bombs made our speed imperative."

Marian remembers the feeling of comradeship which was so strong that many took comfort in each others' arms. "I saw the battery sergeant major, a tough little regular, with his ATS counterpart, searching the camp and surroundings with torches for love nests. Here there was a large number of Americans, and no doubt strictures came down from on high that the protection of British maidenhood required extra vigilance."

Who are we to act as God ?

BACK in London, a dilemma faced the Air Ministry and MI5. The Germans were telling their supposed agents, whom they thought were freely operating in Britain, to report the times and places of flying bomb incidents in London. Truthful information, it was decided, would aid the enemy but false information could be checked by German photographic reconnaissance, in which case the agents would be "blown". The man in charge of scientific intelligence, Dr R.V.Jones takes up the story.

"I had noticed that in the Peenemunde trials the bombs tended to fall short of the target, and now knew that......the operational bombs were also tending to fall short, the centre of gravity being in south-east London, near Dulwich. In a flash I saw that we might be able to keep the bombs falling short, which would mean fewer casualties in London, and at the same time avoid arousing any suspicion regarding...our agents.

"We could give correct points of impact for bombs that tended to have a longer range than usual, but couple these with times of bombs which had fallen short....Therefore, if they made any correction at all, it would be to reduce the average range."

Dr Jones recommended this course of action to "George", with whom he had been involved in supplying misleading information to the Germans but in doing so he realised he was keeping the mean point of impact in Dulwich, where his own parents lived and where he went to school. But he knew that neither his parents nor school would have it otherwise. "George" adopted the plan.

The idea reached political level and both Mr Sandys and Lord Cherwell supported it, but Home Secretary, Herbert Morrison, whose constituency was in Lambeth, thought

Temporary accommodation was found for the patients while the nurses of Lewisham Hospital continued with the task of clearing rubble and debris from the ward which was blasted by the flying bomb of July 26. It was a familiar scenario that summer, for 76 London hospitals were damaged, involving the loss of some 8,200 beds. Altogether 138 patients were killed in hospitals and 1,155 injured — many of them casualties from earlier incidents. The St Helier Hospital at Carshalton was struck twice. The first V1 landed on the morning of Thursday June 21 and injured many nurses who became patients in their own hospital. Six days later it was struck again, killing two people.

the attempt to keep the aiming point short was an effort by Government officials and others in Westminster, Belgravia and Mayfair to "keep the bombs off themselves at the expense of the proletariat in south London".

Dr Jones said: "I was not present at the meeting at which the deception policy was discussed but Herbert Morrison was in the chair and he ruled that it would be an interference with Providence if we were to supply the Germans with misleading information, because this might mean that some people would be killed through our action who might otherwise have survived — overlooking the fact that what we were hoping

to do, would also enable more to survive who might otherwise have been killed."

"George" told Dr Jones of the ruling and asked what he should do. The scientist said he was not at the meeting and until he received instructions in writing, he must continue as they had started.

The deception worked brilliantly but Morrison still went to some lengths to denounce the idea and said that if it had come out into the open there might have been the most serious political circumstances. Later he wrote: "Who are we to act as God?"

"We were soon at work with our jet which I was directing down into what looked like a little bit of hell. Beneath me was swirling, curling smoke, black, brown and other colours and, like all smoke, dirty and stinking. Flames were leaping everywhere and seemed to be doing their best to reach me on the ladder. Intermittently a drum of paint or spirit would explode and shower coloured flames everywhere."

London fireman describing the fire, caused by a doodlebug crashing onto a factory at Great Eastern Street, near Liverpool Street station

West Ham Borough Council's Electricity Department on the junction of Romford Road and Vicarage Lane was hit in the early hours of July 2, completely destroying the southern end of the building. Two weeks later, on July 19, a flying bomb landed on exactly the same spot — again in the early hours of the morning. In each case more than 100 houses were damaged.

THE 55,000 members of the London Fire Brigade, with memories of the Blitz still very clear, found the doodlebug days difficult, unpleasant and exhausting but less of a problem than the "firing" of London in December, 1940.

Even so there were thousands of incidents to attend to and many fires; spectacular fires like the burning of the South Metropolitan Gas Company in east Greenwich and the OK Sauce factory in Wandsworth, terrifying fires like those at the docks where ammunition and petrol cans were stored, repulsive fires where charred limbs had to be removed in sacks and fires at paintworks, schools, churches, factories, workshops, and garages.

Outside London, especially in Kent, the flying bombs caused more destruction than conflagrations. The National Fire Service had excellent communications, great mobility, good equipment and a dogged determination that had served so well during the period of high explosive and incendiary raids. Wherever flying bombs fell they joined civil defence workers in digging out trapped people, covering damaged homes with tarpaulins and making safe potential fire risks. The fire-fighters often risked their own lives in shattered buildings to assist the victims.

Elmers End bus garage after its direct hit on July 17. Altogether there were more than 250 separate incidents affecting London Transport, with many lives lost. On one occasion, at Waterloo, two double-deckers had their tops sliced off and, near the Oval, two trams and two buses crowded with people going home from work, were blown to pieces. By the end of August, few London buses had windows, for what had not been blown out by blast, had been removed to save passengers from being showered with glass splinters. Travelling by bus in the summer of 1944 was not popular — but, for many Londoners, it was the only way to get to work.

Petrol tanks exploded

THE photograph on page 91 shows the remains of the Elmers End bus garage, near Beckenham, after it had received a direct hit on the evening of July 17. About a dozen London Transport staff were in the entrance of the garage when they heard a doodlebug cut out. Everyone scattered. The bomb exploded near the entrance, wrecking the ticket office, canteen, ARP stores and mess room. Six people who went to the kit room were killed instantly and a woman conductor died in another area.

After the explosion, which occurred about 8.30 pm a furious blaze broke out among the debris of the bus garage and the petrol tank of a parked bus exploded. Within minutes the fire had spread and other petrol tanks were blowing up, one by one. The London Fire Brigade appeared quickly on the scene, in time for more explosions. Tyres smouldered, debris was scattered everywhere and bodies were strewn across the kit room.

In all there were 18 fatalities at Elmers End, including the London Transport employees who died instantly in the blast, two members of the Home Guard, a heavy rescue worker, a 74-year-old woman in the street and another woman in a nearby street shelter. There were also more than 40 injuries. The firemen had a particularly hazardous time. With tanks exploding and a fierce fire raging, they had to remove stored petrol and Home Guard ammunition from the garage. A number of firemen were badly injured.

Urgent telephone calls to other garages enabled Elmers End to borrow buses and tickets and next morning the service was resumed as normal, except that some buses had no windows or destination blinds. It was a remarkable achievement in the face of such appalling havoc, for 27 double-deckers, two single deckers and ten ambulances had been destroyed.

There were many other bus incidents. In Battersea, a V1 hit a lorry on Lavender Hill and killed 14 people on a No 77 that was passing at the time. The Battersea garage was damaged three times in two weeks, Camberwell tram depot received four flying bombs and the West Ham depot was hit twice. The first was on July 23 when a large number of trolley buses was damaged but, within 13 hours of the incident, services were operating as normal. In Snaresbrook Road, Wanstead 15 buses were destroyed and on July 27, at Forest Gate, a trolley bus was destroyed and both driver and conductor killed.

A Mustang pilot on constant Diver duty in July was Warrant Officer Tadeusz Szymanski, whose doodlebug heroics with 316 Squadron included a frantic chase above the Kent countryside on the evening of July 12. Szymanski, out of ammunition, flew alongside to get a close look. "The thing was jerking along and the elevator was flapping with each vibration of the crude jet motor", he said. "I noticed that on the front of the bomb was a silly little propeller. It looked ridiculous. I decided to tip it off balance." Wing under wing, stick to starboard but, alas, his adversary proved to be stubborn as a mule. Szymanski was more stubborn. He repeated the manoeuvre eleven times but still they flew on in total harmony until a balloon barrage loomed right in front. "I tried a different manoeuvre, hitting very hard with my wing tip as I went into a loop. When I recovered I found to my dismay it was still flying but I had turned it upside down." Suddenly it plunged to earth in a steep spin and the Polish ace, contented at last, set course for West Malling. Szymanski went on to intercept many more V1s and his heroics earned him the admiration of Polish leader General Sikorski. Tadeusz Szymanski's Mustang (pictured above) bore the name of his daughter, Halinka and shows the number of his successes. Later in life, Tadek (as he was known) and his family settled in Norwich and he became a printer with Jarrolds. He died in February 1992.

The witch hunt

THE July phase of the anti-Diver battle was the most intense. The strain on the airmen who spearheaded it was shown by the rapid turn-round in squadrons. There were bases at Deanland, Ford, Holmesby, Middle Wallop and Brenzett but it was West Malling and Newchurch which were to gain recognition as the foremost airfields on doodlebug duty. The greatest number of bombs crossed the coast at Dungeness, so the emphasis on air defence was placed there with 150 Tempest Wing at Newchurch, the Mustangs of 129 Squadron and 315 (Polish) Squadron operating from Brenzett and the night-fighting Mosquitoes of 96 Squadron at Ford. Further inland, at West Malling, 316 (City of Warsaw) Squadron flew the Mustang alongside 322, 157, 274, 85 and 80, who came and went on brief, but hectic courses of duty.

Squadron Leader Bohdan Arct, leader of 316 (City of Warsaw) Squadron had another name for the V1's. "As they crackled overhead", he said, "they seemed to laugh at us. We called them witches." He recalled how the repulsive sound of passing missiles was accompanied by the roar of the guns and quite often shell splinters rained on their heads. An order was issued to wear steel helmets but the Poles were reluctant to obey it. "The anti-aircraft batteries disturbed us considerably", he said. "The gunners knew very well the silhouettes of flying bombs and our own fighter planes but sometimes they lost their heads. Often we would fly into a cloud of our own artillery bursts and, on one occasion, a medium calibre battery fired so accurately that my wings became perforated and resembled a hunk of Swiss cheese."

Squadron Leader Arct remembers how he was preparing for a patrol when his mechanic said: "Look, sir, here comes a flying witch". Said Arct: "Before I could taxi to the runway it was already overhead. It spluttered its horrid laughter as if saying — 'go on catch me now, you idiot'. When I was at last in the air all I could see was a microscopic dot on the horizon".

The Poles had the last laugh. By the end of July, 316 Squadron had claimed 50 destroyed and moved to a coastal airfield at Friston to chase and "break the bloody backs of more flying witches".

Meanwhile at Newchurch, under the fearless leadership of Roland Beamont, the Tempest V was having even greater success. Up to 50 sorties a day were flown by each of the two Tempest squadrons and pilots' individual scores of two or three V1's in a day were becoming frequent. In mid-July, with 150 Wing approaching its 500th V1 destroyed, the fighter controllers based at Maidstone and Horsham threw a party at Bexhill in honour of Beamont and his men. 150 returned the compliment on July 20, with a "doodlebug dance" at Folkestone. On August 23, Roland Beamont shot down his 30th and last V1, the 632nd to be destroyed by his Wing.

One of the greatest hazards which faced the pilots at Newchurch was the night patrol against the flying bomb. One man, however, enjoyed the challenge so much that he became the greatest doodlebug ace of them all. Squadron Leader Joseph Berry shot down seven in a hectic night of non-stop action on July 23, and by the end of August he had destroyed more than 60. After the campaign was over, Berry was shot down by AA fire over the Dutch coast and killed.

Two airmen who flew on night sorties from Cambridge had a special reason for wanting to stop the V1's from reaching England. One was a pilot whose wife and children had nearly been killed when one fell on their house and the other was a navigator whose mother lived directly beneath the regular flight path.

In the early hours of July 26, 1944, flying over the English Channel in their Mosquito, they were informed that a V1 had been spotted and they were to destroy it. Their progress was followed on the radar screen at operational headquarters — a tiny blob of light which flashed, faded slowly and flashed again. Then, with the Mosquito flying at a height of 7,000 feet and some 25 miles northeast of Margate, the flashing light suddenly disappeared from the screen. No-one really knew what happened but it was assumed that they had collided with their target.

The navigator who died was 20-year-old James Farrar and few people realised just how great a loss England and the world of literature had suffered by the death of this young man. Had he lived he would certainly have become famous as a poet and novelist. A notebook in which he recorded his personal thoughts and experiences, sprinkled with stories and verse was published in 1950 under the title *The Unreturning Spring*.

The Tempest

A Tempest V at Newchurch, on Romney Marsh during the flying bomb campaign. In 1944 the Tempest Vs were the fastest propeller-driven fighters below 20,000 feet in operational service on either side. The smaller picture shows a Tempest closing in on its prey but Wing Commander Roland Beamont said there was a danger in getting too close. "On one occasion a flying bomb was exploded by cannon fire from 200 yards away. The Tempest concerned went straight through the fireball and returned safely but streaked with smoke and evidence of charring on the elevators and on the rudder."

THE GENIUS OF JAMES FARRAR

James Farrar, the young navigator who was killed while attempting to destroy a flying bomb, was only 20 when he died, but he left behind poems, stories and sketches which show him to have been one of the most promising writers of his generation. These were published in 1950 in a book titled *The Unreturning Spring*. The editor, Henry Wilkinson in an introduction about James Farrar wrote: "In his letters burns the many coloured flame of genius, now tender, now fierce, sometimes meditative, sometimes light-hearted, but always the master of beautiful language."

AFTER NIGHT OFFENSIVE

Glowed through the violet petal of the sky
Like a death's-head the calm summer moon
And all the distance echoed with owl-cry

Hissing the white waves of grass unsealed
Peer of moon on metal, hidden men,
As the wind foamed deeply through the field.

Rooted to soil, remote and faint as stars,
Looking to neither side, they lay all night
Sunken in the murmurous seas of grass.

No flare burned upwards: never sound was shed
But lulling cries of owls beyond the world
As wind and moon played softly with the dead.

James Farrar, who disappeared over the Channel, chasing a V1.

THE DAILY MAIL, Tuesday July 25, 1944

Beamont—first fly-bomb ace

By Daily Mail Reporter

Britain's first ace flying bomb killer has won another award, it is announced today.

He is acting Wing Commander Roland Beamont and he wins a Bar to his D.S.O. He also holds the D.F.C. and Bar.

Although the citation makes no mention of his successes against flying bombs, it is known that Wing Commander Beamont, in recent weeks, has shot many of the bombs down into the sea.

Wing Commander Beamont is a former test pilot, and at 25, commands a station from which the Tempest, fastest aeroplane in the world, operates.

He comes from Chichester and is known as Britain's ace loco-buster.

Permanent duty

He is more or less on permanent duty against the flying bomb, I was told last night. He is never far from his fighter and volunteers to go up as soon as his station plotters locate the bomb.

"We have plenty of good marksmen here, hence our success", he told me.

"Some of us have had queer experiences with flying bombs. We've come back spattered with black oil all over our machines, with fuselage singed, and even with rudders burnt off.

"We do all sorts of things to them — blow their wings off, shoot their engines away, fire their fuel which sets their bombs off. During one period we knocked down four out of five."

The story which appeared in The Daily Mail on July 25, 1944 about Roland Beamont. After the war Beamont became a leading Test Pilot and an immensely respected figure in aviation circles.

This is the photograph which appeared in the Daily Mirror almost two weeks after the incident at Leytonstone. Eileen Clements was the then anonymous 11-year-old girl being carried to safety in the arms of a fireman from the wreckage of her home.

Carried to safety in the arms of a fireman

THE photograph on the left of a little girl being rescued from the wreckage of her home is one that has been used time and again to symbolise the days when the doodlebug was at its most menacing. It first appeared in the *Daily Mirror* and shows 11-year-old Eileen Clements being carried in the arms of a fireman from No 5 Arundel Road, a terraced house in Leytonstone.

Eileen, aged 11, was playing in the street on the evening of Monday July 24 when the flying bomb came over. She ran to the Anderson shelter and dived in just as there was a tremendous crash. The explosion flung her to the far end of the shelter. Her sister, Lily, aged 18, was in the bedroom, combing her hair in the wardrobe mirror. The house collapsed in the impact, the wardrobe fell over and Lily was trapped underneath, but shielded from falling plaster and debris. The view outside was horrific. The row of terraced houses had disintegrated and a massive pall of smoke and dust hung in the air.

In Leytonstone town centre, Eileen and Lily's parents, Alfred and Thirza, were at the cinema when the explosion occurred. The film stopped, the audience rushed out and the couple ran frantically home as fire engines approached. When they reached Arundel Road, they found it had been roped off, and the sight that greeted them was a massive pile of jagged timber and masonry; in fact the whole street had collapsed.

Rescue workers were already there. They had lifted a shocked and bruised Eileen from the shelter and joined the firemen from Leyton in digging Lily from the rubble. Leading Fireman Bill Sayers carried Eileen to safety for a tearful reunion with her parents, who minutes later learned that Lily was also alive.

The photograph was used in the *Daily Mirror* a few days later. There was no reference to the identity of the girl, or the locality but a story, accompanying the picture said that 17,000 homes had been destroyed and 800,000 damaged by flying bombs — and still they kept coming. "Where can the luckless, the threatened and the homeless go?", asked the Mirror. "Homes are wanted desperately."

Eileen Alexander (née Clements) has never forgotten the day she was carried from the debris of her home in Leytonstone. She still remembers the silence of the engine cutting out, the blast that followed, the smell of brick, dust and soot, the absolute despair of people emerging from their shelters and the bravery of the firemen, police and wardens.

Following her appearance on the BBC TV programme, London Plus some years ago, a viewer rang Eileen to give the name of the fireman, Bill Sayers, whom she had never met. Sadly he had died but she met his widow and that, she says, was a very moving experience. A painting of Eileen appears on the dust cover of the third volume of the magnificent trilogy on the Blitz, produced by "After The Battle". The editor, Winston G Ramsey, in dedicating this volume to the victims, also invited Eileen to write the foreword. In 1992, when her photograph (left) was taken, she was living at Wickford in Essex.

KENT MESSENGER   FRIDAY JULY 21, 1944

GUN-FIRE BAPTISMS IN ATHOL TERRACE

Front-line kiddies have never slept in their own cots

Children are still being born and brought up in a row of houses, Athol Terrace, Dover, which faces across the Channel to enemy occupied France.

Nestling between the towering white cliffs, Athol Terrace is in all England the inhabited place which is nearest the enemy.

It is the hottest part of Hell's Corner !

And when the history of Dover's part in the war comes to be written a proud place will be given to the mothers of Athol Terrace. Five years of terror have failed to drive them from their homes. They are still rearing families of healthy and happy children.

Many of the children born in Athol Terrace since the war began have never known what it is to sleep in a bed in their own homes.

Each evening when bedtime comes the mothers, instead of taking the children upstairs and tucking them in their cots, take them along to the deep caves which honeycomb the cliffs.

Typical of the front-line mothers is Mrs Mary Culley, of 4 Athol Terrace. Up to the war she had one son, Bombardier Jack Culley who is with the Royal Artillery in Gibraltar.

After the birth of Jack she went 15 years without any more children. Then on April 23, 1941, a little boy, Michael was born. On March 20, 1942, Kathleen entered the world of explosions and now Mrs Culley has a baby in arms, Patricia, born on March 17 this year.

The children of Athol Terrace do not know what it is like to be afraid of the dark. They toddle around the dark caves as cheerfully as an ordinary child would run down the passage of a house.

This is the story which appeared on the front page of the County Edition of the Kent Messenger on July 21, 1944. The photograph shows Mr and Mrs Culley with their three children Patricia, Kathleen and Michael at the entrance to the caves above Athol Terrace, Dover. In the next column is a heavily-censored story of flying bombs which were shot down over "Southern England" watched by thousands of people. "Children, waiting in a queue, were among those killed by one which crashed in a street and struck a shop", said the newspaper.

Swanscombe's turn again

SWANSCOMBE'S place in the history of the flying bomb campaign was already assured with the first to crash on British soil in mid-June. Although that one fell harmlessly in a potato field it reminded villagers what might have been and they anxiously watched or listened every day and night, silently uttering the words that were on everyone's lips at the time — "keep going, you bugger, keep going".

On Sunday July 30 at 11.30 am, women came out of their kitchens and men, in their gardens or allotments looked up as the menacing drone was heard again. The engine cut out and the missile fell onto Taunton Road in the village centre with an earth-shattering explosion which echoed for many miles around. It was one of North Kent's most serious incidents; 13 people killed, 22 seriously injured and 69 slightly hurt. There was damage to almost 100 properties and, on this peaceful summer Sunday morning, Swanscombe was transformed into a scene of pandemonium. The serious cases were taken to Gravesend Hospital. The first-aid post at Northfleet paper mills dealt with the non-serious. Rest centres were opened at Lawn Road School in Northfleet and the Southfleet Road Central School at Southfleet.

Eight houses in the village were completely demolished and more than 150 people were made homeless. Among them were two Royal Marine sergeants, home on leave after taking part in the Normandy landings. They were blown from a window by the blast onto the street below. One regained consciousness to find himself in the street surrounded by rubble. His wife and two children had reached the shelter and were unhurt.

One eye-witness, a Mr Everdale, was standing in a field beyond the village when he saw a doodlebug being chased by fighters. "The flying bomb began to lose altitude and I thought it would crash in the fields but it hit the village", he recalled. Another to have a narrow escape was a local dairy farmer who was loading up his milk delivery van when he heard the missile cut-out. He dived under a haystack and escaped unhurt. His van was demolished.

Furniture is salvaged from damaged homes. This is Swanscombe village on July 30, 1944.

The children of St. John's School, Shirley had heard the air-raid warning and were in the shelter when the bomb fell. They were unhurt, as were the occupants of the cottages just 10 yards from where the missile impacted. They were said to have emerged hysterical and covered in dust.

Shirley school demolished

THE villages surrounding Croydon, and the town itself, were still in the centre of the bombardment and, by late July, flying bombs were falling with devastating regularity. Many were actually brought down by the balloon barrage near Sevenoaks, for those that got caught in the cables often limped on for a few miles, losing height and momentum, only to crash in the borough of Croydon.

The photograph above shows the ruins of the village school at Shirley which received a direct hit on July 26. The blast damaged many houses, including the two school cottages and took part of the roof off St John's parish church. The loss of the school involved numerous complications for the church and took ten years to resolve. The church was restored in 1947.

One who witnessed this, and many other incidents in Surrey is John Rawlings, now of Lewes, Sussex whose father was vicar of Shirley in 1944. John writes: "My youth was spent in Shirley vicarage in an area which provided a front-line view of the Battle of Britain, the blitz, doodlebugs and rockets. We suffered severe damage from bombs, incendiaries and, worst of all, flying bombs. Our church was damaged by these and the school demolished.

On one occasion, whilst helping the verger to dig a grave (one of my wartime activities) we counted 17 flying bombs approaching in line—abreast, some gliding, some diving and some under power. If hit, we thought at least we could save anyone the job of burying us.

As a member of the Home Guard I spent much time helping civilians to clear rubble and salvage belongings from destroyed homes. Nearly 4,000 doodlebugs were destroyed by AA guns and fighters but unfortunately the balloon barrage at Sevenoaks tended to merely interfere with the flight of these missiles so that they could just about reach the Croydon area."

Many flying bombs managed to slip between the balloon cables and chug on towards London; others, spitting furiously, struggled forward for a few miles and dived to earth near towns like Croydon. This one was splendidly caught by the balloon at Meopham, exploded on striking the cable and impacted in a nearby field, uncomfortably close to the balloon site at Shipley Hills Road. The balloon crew were quick to inspect their first victim.

FIGHTERS WHICH HUNTED THE V1

Aircraft	Engine	Armament	Speed 2,000ft	Squadrons
Hawker Tempest V	2,400hp Napier Sabre 11 B	Four 20 mm cannon	420 mph	Nos 3, 486, 56, 274, 501 with NFDU
Vickers Supermarine Spitfire F-XIV	2,000 hp Rolls Royce Griffon 65	Two 20mm cannon and four 0.303inchMG	385mph	Nos 91, 322
North American Mustang 111 (P-51B/C)	1,380 hp Packard Merlin V-1650-3	Six 0.50in MG	375mph	The Polish Wing with 316
Gloster Meteor	Two 1,700lb st Rolls-Royce Welland 1	Four 20mm cannon	485mph	No 616
D.H.Mosquito Various marks	Two 1,390hp Rolls-Royce Merlin 23	Four 20mm cannon	365mph	Nos 25, 68, 85, 96 125, 157, 219, 409, 418 at various times

Meteor joins the fray

ON August 4, 1944, Flying Officer Dixie Dean of 616 Squadron took off from Manston on anti-Diver duty to patrol an inland area under Biggin Hill control. At 16.16 hours he sighted a flying bomb at 1,000 feet, dived down at a speed of 450 mph and attacked the missile from dead astern. His 20mm cannons failed to fire owing to a technical fault so Dean flew alongside, manoeuvered his wing tip a few inches under the wing of the flying bomb, pulled upwards sharply and sent the bomb diving to earth south of Tonbridge.

This report in Operations Record Book of 616 Squadron is part of aviation history. Dean was flying the twin-engine Gloster Meteor, the first high-performance jet fighter in RAF Fighter Command and had become the first jet pilot to destroy a flying bomb.

The Meteors had come into operational service at the end of July and 616 Squadron, based at Manston, had been given the honour of baptising them. It was the afternoon of August 4 that seven Meteors were scrambled and Dean's success was followed, at 16.40, by Flying Officer J.K.Rodger who fired two bursts at a flying bomb and saw it crash five miles north-west of Tenterden.

Tram queue in Lordship Lane

BY August some 50 per cent of the flying bombs were being destroyed before they could reach London but those that beat the defences continued to cause heavy casualties and damage. In the first week, 395 were killed in London and 57 elsewhere. There were big fires at West Ham on August 1 and Greenwich on the 3rd. On August 5, a bomb crashed onto the Royal Arsenal Co-operative Stores at Lordship Lane, Camberwell. The shop, crowded with customers, was demolished and a tram queue outside was cut to pieces. Twenty three people died and 43 were injured.

In the second week of August — the ninth of the campaign — 459 flying bombs were reported, a figure that increased to 700 in the third week and 550 in the fourth.

In Kent, during the month, there were flying bomb fatalities in Maidstone, Horsmonden, Littlebourne, Snodland, Tunbridge Wells, Dartford, Swanscombe(again), Boughton Monchelsea, Benenden, Ightham, Hythe, Appledore, Newington, Strood, Otford, Dover and Smarden. In Sussex, there were fatalities at Laughton, Pevensey, Bexhill and Hartfield.

In one incident, at Frinsted, near Hollingbourne, a flying bomb which exploded in a field contained cannisters carrying German propaganda leaflets. These showed gruesome pictures of victims of an Allied raid on Cologne. The cannisters were taken to Sittingbourne police station, and then on to London.

One of the worst incidents was on August 23 at East Barnet when the premises of the Standard Telephone and Cable Company were hit and 21 people died.

Maidstone misery: 3 in a day

Three flying bombs fell in, or near, Maidstone on Thursday August 3. The first dived onto the golf course in the early hours of the morning, seriously injuring three women, slightly hurting 11 other people and damaging 450 houses. The second, just before noon, exploded in the goods yard of Maidstone West railway station. Five men were killed, five women and five men seriously injured and 40 people slightly hurt. Gas supplies and telephone lines were wrecked and 1,180 homes damaged. On that same day a third bomb crashed at nearby Allington, causing more damage.

A flying bomb, shot down by a fighter, crashed in Malling Road, Snodland at 6.58 pm on Saturday August 5, demolishing ten houses and damaging many more. Twelve people were killed and 16 seriously injured. The Kent Messenger reported that two local doctors displayed great heroism despite being injured themselves. One, a Czech refugee, was holding his surgery when the bomb fell. He was badly cut in the face by glass splinters and bleeding heavily but he continued to do what he could for those who had been hurt. The other doctor, who was in the front room of his house, received the full force of the blast and was thrown against the man he was treating. Although his leg was broken he also continued to treat the injured.

Among those killed was a nine-year-old girl, who was a patient at the surgery, a police sergeant, his wife and two girls, who were staying with the doctor, and several neighbours.

Mr Derek Pantony, of Whitstable was crossing an open field at Coxheath, near Maidstone when he saw this flying bomb tipped over by a Tempest. It veered to port before crashing in Snodland. Mr Pantony writes: "The pilot was heavily criticised at the time for employing this well-known tactic but from my position it was clear that if he had opened fire it is highly likely that it would have crashed in the centre of Maidstone, where the casualty rate may have been much higher. I feel the pilot was unjustifiably pilloried."

Front Line Anglia

"EXCEPT possibly for a few last shots, the Battle of London is over." With these words Mr Duncan Sandys spoke with great confidence about the immediate future to a crowded press conference on September 7. He said that during the 80 days of the bombardment the Germans had sent over some 8,000 flying bombs of which 2,300 had got through to London. "The understanding and restraint of the people living in Kent, Sussex and Surrey are deserving of great praise. By their readiness to accept their share of London's dangers, the people of Bomb Alley played a notable part in keeping down overall casualties."

Mr Sandys had a special word of praise for the Americans. "They have thrown themselves into the job of beating the bomb with just as much determination as if New York or Washington had been the victim of the attack."

He mentioned the possibility that the missiles might now be launched from aircraft. Mr Sandys had firm evidence that a new attack from the east was being organised from Heinkel 111s or Junkers 88s. but he knew there were considerable fears among German officers about the inaccuracy of air-launched Vls — a fear that was to prove well founded.

On September 14 after an interval of some days, the air-launched attacks were renewed in a line over East Anglia to the north of the small anti-aircraft 'Diver box' which had covered the approaches to the capital from the east. In consultation with Fighter Command, AA Command decided to redeploy all the available defences from the South Coast in a strip 5,000 yards wide extending from the Thames Estuary to Great Yarmouth. It was another mammoth operation in which great convoys of 10 ton lorries moved guns and gunners to their new positions. By the middle of October, 300 static guns, 542 heavy guns, 503 40-mm guns and 18 searchlight batteries were achieving further high successes.

The gunners had to learn a new technique for destroying low-flying air launched Vl's but, despite the autumn weather which was particularly wet, morale was high and the percentage of "kills" rose eventually to 82. During this period 13 flying bombs landed in Norfolk, injuring 11 people. No-one was killed.

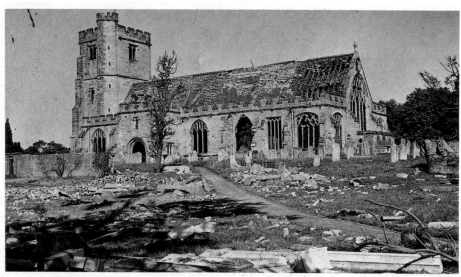

On the day that Duncan Sandys held his press conference and mentioned the possibility of air-launched V1s being aimed at London, one was actually spotted, chased and shot down by a fighter over Kent. It landed in Hawkhurst churchyard, uprooting tombstones and causing great damage to the church.

Duck-boards across the mud

ALTHOUGH winter had not yet begun, conditions on the new gun sites in Essex and East Anglia were appalling. One visitor, concerned about the conditions under which men and women were living and fighting was the Speaker of the House of Commons. In his report he said:

"It reminded me of Flanders in the last war, but the mud was not quite so sticky. The gun crews were living in tents, the men were on the alert all night, so little could be done by day. But they had erected duck-board passages across the mud which I thought was highly creditable." The Speaker explained how, in ten minutes, he saw two doodlebugs out of three shot down over the coast and the third probably winged. "Not bad shooting under such conditions."

By now there was great controversy over the plight that faced the ATS girls, who, nevertheless, were proud that they were allowed to "rough it" with the men. One mixed battery at Burnham lived in tents surrounded by quagmires. Even hardened gunners complained, so the brigadier offered to transfer the 1,000 girls of the brigade to other, more comfortable sites.

He received nine applications — all from clerks. The ATS girls in the front line of the anti-aircraft campaign all volunteered to remain on the unwelcoming marshes of Essex, and fight the battle with the men.

The Battle of London is over! This welcome news, far too premature as events turned out, spread like wildfire across England and within days of the announcement evacuees came flooding back gleefully, many to their deaths — for soon to arrive from the east was Hitler's deadliest weapon of all, the V2. The photograph here shows a group of children who had been as far away as possible from the flying bombs.   They landed at Southampton on September 11 after a long sea voyage from Australia on RMS Andes.

First rocket lands in Paris

BY the beginning of September, 1944 the Nazis were ready at last for the rocket offensive. The A4 became known as the V2, or Vergeltungswaffe-zwei (vengeance weapon two) and two batteries were moved into position for firing — one directed at Paris and the second at London. By this time all northern France and most of Belgium had been liberated by the Allies and what remained of the prepared rocket-launching sites in Pas de Calais was now the tramping ground of Allied troops. Hitler's orders were to attack Paris first and Batterie 444 positioned itself at Euskirchen, 15 miles south west of Bonn while the 2nd Batterie of Artillery Detachment 485 of Gruppe Nord moved into The Hague to prepare for a double launch against London.

On Wednesday September 6 two V2s were aligned with Paris and eight tons of volatile fuel were pumped into each. The first was ignited shortly after 9 am but the motor cut out just as it was about to lift off. The rocket fell back onto the firing table where it tottered but remained upright. The same happened with the second rocket some 40 minutes later. So far the V2 rocket assault was more like a damp squib!

The technicians discovered the fault and by dawn on Thursday morning were ready to fire again. The first rocket lifted off haphazardly and disappeared into the distance never to be seen again; the second was a perfect launch. It rose into the stratosphere and five minutes later came down to earth in the Paris suburb of Maisons Alfort, killing six people.

Three more shots were fired at Paris, a distance of 200 miles, but the Americans were advancing so fast that the detachment had to withdraw from Euskirchen and join the batteries at The Hague for the attack on Britain. Paris was spared.

Death from the stratosphere

THERE was a great air of optimism in London and south-east England on Friday September 8, despite the false news of the German surrender three days earlier. The Allied armies were rolling inexorably eastwards through Belgium and towards the borders of Adolf Hitler's Fatherland. Everywhere there was serious talk of the end of the war before Christmas. After five years of hardship, ending with those terrible doodlebugs, the end of hostilities was now a reality.

As the people of London dispersed from their offices, shops and factories on this fine autumn evening with the weekend ahead, they were blissfully ignorant of the fact that fifty miles above the earth a long dark rocket, weighing 13 tons, armed with a ton of high explosive, travelling at more than 3,000 mph was hurtling towards London from the Dutch coast. No-one heard it, no-one saw it.

At 6.43 pm the rocket ended its brief but deadly flight, plummeting from the

This was Staveley Road, Chiswick after the first V2 had exploded. Three people were killed, Mrs Ada Harrison and a little girl from next door, Rosemary Clarke, aged three. The third victim was army private Frank Browning who was crossing the road when the rocket fell. Germany made no formal announcement of the incident and the British Government, meeting without Churchill who was on his way to Canada, imposed a total news black-out.

....four times the speed of sound

stratosphere at four times the speed of sound into the ground in the western suburb of Chiswick. The explosion in Staveley Road created a 30-foot wide crater. Three people died, 17 were seriously injured, six houses were totally destroyed and many others severely damaged. As the missile impacted into the concrete, a thunderous explosion echoed right across London; there was immediate confusion for no-one had heard the sound of a German bomber or the drone of a flying bomb, or an air-raid alert. Those living in West London heard a double thunderclap, after the impact — the noise of the rocket breaking the sound barrier.

This was the turning point in the history of warfare. The V2 rocket offensive had begun and from this moment in time military strategy

was revolutionised. Chiswick in West London was the first place in England to be introduced to the long-range ballistic missile.

There followed a conspiracy of silence. The question on everyone's lips remained unanswered for several weeks. The official euphemism for this and the following explosions was that gas mains had blown up. Those who felt the pavement shake under their feet, looked up to see a white vapour trail hanging vertically in the air and then heard the double boom, were more sceptical. Could this, they wondered, be Hitler's much-vaunted long-range rocket which Duncan Sandys had refused to discuss at his conference a few days earlier? He said he knew about the V2 and in a few days time the press would be walking over the abandoned launching sites in France.

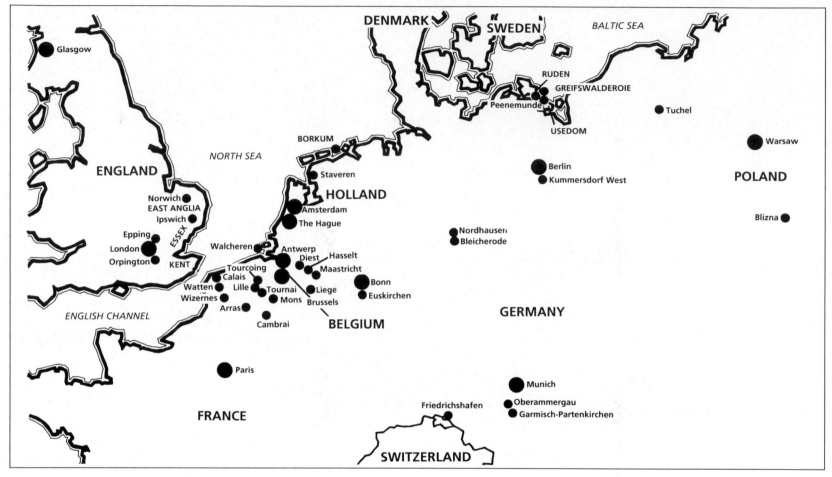

THIS map of Northern Europe and England shows the locations of the principal towns in the V2 campaign. By the time the first missile was launched, France and most of Belgium had been liberated and two of the rocket assembly plants, at **Watten** and **Wizernes** in Pas de Calais, overrun by the advancing troops. Watten, in fact, was the world's largest bunker and 130,000 tons of concrete went into its construction. The heavy Allied bombing could only knock a few lumps out of its vast walls.

It was from **Euskirchen**, south of Bonn, that the first rocket was fired at Paris. The Germans then withdrew to **The Hague** and **Walcheren Island** where they joined the other batteries for the attack on England. From here, the first two rockets fell at **Chiswick** and **Epping**. On September 25 an attack was opened on a number of Continental targets, notably **Antwerp, Brussels, Liege** and **Lille.** It was on that day that rockets were fired from **Staveren** in Friesland towards targets in **East Anglia**.

Other locations on this map include **Kummersdorf West**, south of Berlin, where the German Army Weapons Department was first established, **Peenemunde**, where the missile was developed, **Blizna** and then **Tuchel**, the firing ranges in Poland and **Nordhausen**, where the V2 was assembled in vast factories under the Harz mountains.

The little town of **Oberammergau** has yet to figure in the V2 story, but it was to this peaceful spot in the Bavarian Alps that the rocket men eventually moved.

The "flying gas mains"

Dr Jones and his colleague in Scientific Intelligence, Charles Frank were in their office at the Air Ministry when they heard a double bang. The two men looked at each other and said almost simultaneously — "that's the first one". A few moments later came another boom made by a missile on its supersonic descent. This one had landed at Parndon Wood, near Epping.

The two incidents made a complete mockery of the day's headlines which had actually proclaimed the end of the flying bomb battle. They also coincided with the news that the Allied armies were held up in their advance across Belgium by the rivers Scheldt and Rhine, and so there was an area around the Hook of Holland still in German hands — an area destined to remain so throughout the winter.

The third V2, on September 10, came down at Fambridge, near Southend, the fourth blew up in a field at Crockenhill, near Swanley and the fifth at Magdalen Laver. There was little damage and no casualties. On Tuesday September 12 there were four more — at Paglesham, near Rochford, Keston, near Biggin Hill, Dagenham and Kew Gardens. The casualty list so far was eight killed and 28 seriously injured.

There were no official announcements apart from Ministry references to "gas main explosions", which led the public to christen them the "flying gas mains".

The first V2 to fall in Kent was at Field Crouch Farm, Crockenhill. It caused no casualties or damage but brought down thousands of apples from a nearby orchard and gave the farmer his quickest apple picking season ever.

Big bangs attract the 'big noises'

Wednesday September 20: Out of the east came the deep throbbing of a late doodlebug. I was just in time to see the fiery tail swing rapidly sideways and plunge headlong down against a pale white background of searchlights. Control said "Green Man" area of Waltham Cross. I went poste haste to the incident. Confusion reigned for a time, when it seemed that everyone was milling around in all directions. Converted my car into a control point after turning into Eastbrook Road. The bomb had fallen smack into Cobbins Brook. Houses in Honey Lane facing the Larsen Rec were in a sorry state and the damage extended in varying degrees up many roads. All around was the tinkling of glass and the "smack" of tiles falling, and householders were busy sweeping glass and plaster into the roads. 400 houses were affected. Photograph shows the incident post at The Green Man, Bill Beanse looking over the shoulder of Kath Stewart.

EDWARD Carter, Chief Warden for the Urban District of Waltham Holy Cross from 1939 to 1945 kept a diary in which he recorded all the main incidents and took many photographs. Some years after the war the diary was published by Waltham Abbey Historical Society. Here are some extracts beginning on Saturday September 9, 1944 when Ted, like most people, was rather confused by the "mysterious explosions".

Saturday September 9: So now what? Last evening at about 1845 two large explosions heard, but apparently some distance off, though they shook doors and windows. I thought the first one must be thunder, so loud did it seem and so long did it rumble and echo.

At the scene of the incident we found Harris from Group 7, Smith, the bomb recce man and several others. Crater about 8 ft deep and 20 ft across and trees and shrubs all round, just wiped out. Clearly not a PAC, nor Compo, not ordinary bomb. Must be something out of the ordinary to attract all the "big noises". An odd feature is that no-one seems to have heard it coming.

Tuesday September 12: More of the "mysterious missiles" have fallen. They appear to be stratosphere-rocket-shells, possibly launched from Jutland or inside Germany itself. The terrific height and speed at which they travel makes them invisible and inaudible and apparently they travel to earth considerably faster than their own sound.

Wednesday September 13: Went with Ellis to Dagenham this pm to see the effects of a "mysterious missile". Not so bad as I had expected, and not so bad as doodlebug damage.

Thursday September 14: A loud explosion (another gas main!) Fell at Walthamstow right alongside Group 7 HQ. Crater 25 ft deep filling with water from a broken main. Transformer station in the ground of the new Town Hall with walls sucked out and reinforced concrete roof curved down to the ground, all cracked and broken. A long shapeless heap of rubble and dust was all that was left of a row of houses - about 11 in all. Here and there, an odd piece of wall stood dejectedly, and at one end a bedroom opened to the four winds retained its bed and bedding.

Soft 'pop' in Woolwich

I worked for the Ministry of Supply at Woolwich for the whole of the war and experienced more than 60 ordinary bombing raids. Often I had to walk home from Woolwich to Welling because of damage to the tram lines.

It was in September, 1944 that we began to hear loud bangs at intervals and were told that gas mains were exploding in different areas. On the morning of September 14, I was sitting in the kitchen eating my breakfast when there was a soft 'pop' and all the windows shot open. I went into the hall and was aghast to see that the front door was hanging off and the frame was falling outwards. Then the silence ended; the air became dark with debris raining down and I could hear screams.

I had to get to work but my sister and other neighbours helped anyone they could, because a row of houses in Dairsee Road had received a direct hit, killing seven people and injuring dozens of others. A girl I knew had just come back from leave but was met at the station to be told that her mother and sister had been killed. Her father was discovered amid the debris unscathed.

Joan Smith, Tenterden, Kent

A blinding flash from the direction of Central London — the sight often witnessed by Len Northrop.

A blinding flash

The V2's four-minute journey to London was as fast and silent as the fastest shooting star, but without its beauty. Many times in that weary winter of 1944-5, with peace already in the wings, I would walk home at night after going to a cinema at Rochester. When the night was clear and starlit I enjoyed the three-mile stroll and it had the added bonus of keeping me fit for my football games.

On occasions, as I walked the tree-lined route to my village and looked across the darkened hills to London, there would come a blinding flash, silence for perhaps 15 seconds, then a heavy thud that shook the night. Death and destruction from the sky was 30 miles away and here was I on a lonely road thinking of my football game the next day.

Such was the drama of those weeks. The emotions played all kinds of tricks but, to a youth of the time, life was dangerous, dramatic and highly exciting.

Len Northrop, Herstmonceux, Near Hailsham

Doodlebug Alley moves to Essex

THE statement by Mr Duncan Sandys that the flying bomb launching sites in France and Belgium had been captured and the menace was finally over, was premature. As refugees came streaming back, many to roofless houses, Colonel Wachtel's men had regrouped in north-west Germany and were now ready to launch from specially-adapted Heinkel aircraft. Doodlebug Alley was about to move to a new county; Essex was under the direct firing line.

At dawn on Saturday September 16, nine bombs were released. Five were shot down, two crashed in open country and one got through to Woolwich. The ninth fell in St Awdry's Road, Barking, killing 13 people and injuring more than 100.

The following evening the roar of a flying bomb brought hundreds of people into the streets of Colchester. They saw the thrilling sight of a V1 being chased by a fighter. Machine gun fire was heard as it crossed the town followed, a few minutes later, by an explosion as the robot fell harmlessly in a village field.

The *Essex County Standard* reported how another bomb, which fell at Little Baddow, cost the life of Mrs Gregory Nicholson, secretary of the Essex Drama League, whose house was demolished. "The bombs", said the newspaper, "were now flying at a much lower altitude and on September 20 one flew into a hill at Maldon. There were 12 casualties. Among those who escaped were a couple rescued unhurt from a Morrison shelter in a wrecked house.

"During the following week, bombs roared over Colchester every night and in the early hours of September 27 one crashed in Ardleigh, destroying four thatched cottages. Four people were killed — Mrs Ada Cheeseman, her two children and Mr Wilfred Jaggard. The doodlebug was heard approaching the village. Its engine stopped and the inhabitants heard it gliding on. One man described the sound as 'like the whistling of a bomb'. Then there was a terrific bang which seemed to last for more than a minute."

Just before this incident, the villagers of Marks Tey, Copford and Easthorpe had appealed to the Regional Commissioner of the Eastern Civil Defence, requesting that an air raid siren be installed in the vicinity. The appeal, representing 900 residents, was turned down owing to the "limitations of the supply of equipment and the lack of minimum conditions of population density."

In Colchester, flying bomb alerts were now a nightly occurrence. There were explosions at Inworth, Sudbury and Ware and "on the black moonless night of October 5, a robot damaged by anti-aircraft fire, missed houses near the Abbey Field, struck a tree and

Four thatched cottages stood on this site at Ardleigh, near Colchester. They were destroyed on the morning of September 27, 1944. One person was killed.

exploded at Reeds Hall'. The tree in direct line with an army hut crowded with soldiers, probably saved scores of lives.

The village of Marks Tey, its people angry that the petition for a siren had been rejected, was now being peppered with flying bombs. There were no fatalities but many houses, stables, barns and glasshouses were completely wrecked. The railway line was damaged and, on one occasion, customers of the Trowel and Hammer public house were showered with glass.

Air-launched V1s continued to fall in Essex throughout October, November and up to Christmas, 1944, when the Allied occupation of key bases near the German frontier gave Essex a brief respite. In this time, however, the doodlebugs caused considerable damage at Thorrington, Little Bentley, Eight Ash Green (destroying the parish church), Great Bentley, West Mersea and Fingringhoe.

One bomb hit allotments near Berechurch Road, Colchester, demolished a number of houses and blew all the windows out of the Queen's Hotel. The landlord, Mr Joe Girling, twice previously bombed out, opened as usual, selling what he described as "real draught beer".

A bridge too far

FIVE members of one family, the Shins, were killed when a rocket struck their terraced house in Adelaide Avenue, Lewisham on September 17. It was the 25th to reach England — and the worst to date. The blast destroyed 11 homes in the road, 14 people died and 29 were seriously injured.

By this time the Home Office had received serious warnings from British agents on the Continent about the likely severity of the attacks and new stringent precautions were taken to protect Londoners, who would have been shocked if they knew of the plans being made for their safety.

It was decided to select suitable assembly points outside a radius of about five miles from the centre of London. Those refugees escaping on foot would be picked up by buses and transported to these points, which were mostly schools, cinemas, dance halls and football stadiums.

The people of Sidcup, and those who arrived there by bus, would have been required to make their way to the Central School at Alma Road, or to the Odeon Cinema from where they would be driven to Maidstone. The evacuees from Beckenham, so it was planned, would go to the Regal Cinema and then on to Sevenoaks. Bromley and Orpington would also be evacuated to Sevenoaks. Altogether there were 87 top-secret routes in the fringe areas and the picking up points were chosen at random. If the emergency plan had been put into operation the police and the WVS would have played a vital part.

On the same day as the Adelaide Avenue disaster at Lewisham, British airborne forces began landing on their dropping zones at Arnhem in the Allied operation to capture the Rhine Bridges. This heroic operation, code-named "Market Garden" severely threatened Hans Klammer's rocket units who, fearful his men would be cut off, hastily withdrew and the firings ceased for about a week. There was one parting shot. A rocket landed in Chatsworth Way, West Norwood scoring a direct hit on the church. Two died and 51 were injured.

After holding the bridgehead at Arnhem for nine days against overwhelming odds, the British and Polish troops surrendered and the operation was abandoned. On September 25 the rocket attacks re-commenced but the aiming point now was East Anglia, and Norwich appeared to be the centre of the target.

The Wermacht had set up shop in south-west Friesland.

One of the V1 launching sites overrun by Canadian forces sweeping through Holland. This ramp was used to launch flying bombs against Antwerp. Just before pulling out the Germans blew up as many sites and bombs as they could.

Rockets on East Anglia

FEWER than 30 missiles had been launched from the German rocket sites in the suburbs of The Hague and on Walcheren Island before the ill-fated Market Garden operation forced Versuchsbatterie 444 to withdraw. Dr Klammer instructed his unit to move forward to the Gaasterland district of south-west Friesland, where they found an ideal site in a thickly wooded area close to the hamlet of Rijs and well concealed from the prying cameras of Allied reconnaissance aircraft. The V2 had a 200-mile maximum range and the cities of Ipswich and Norwich were the only centres of sizeable population now within firing range.

On the afternoon of Tuesday September 26, the village of Ranworth in Norfolk was shaken by the ear-splitting double explosion which shattered windows for a radius of a half mile from the centre of the blast. The rocket had impacted in a field of stubble, creating a crater 25 feet deep and 40 feet in diameter. A column of black smoke could be seen from Norwich, eight miles away, a clear indication that the V2 offensive had moved into East Anglia.

During the next 16 days more than 30 rockets were destined to land in the two eastern counties and more than a dozen in Essex. For the Rijs rocket team the operation was a complete flop for the missiles repeatedly fell harmlessly in rural areas; there were no fatal casualties and only 51 people were injured — mainly by flying glass.

The worst incident, and one which could have been far more tragic, occurred on October 4 at 1.40 pm when a rocket landed just 100 yards from the village school of Rockland St Mary about five miles from Norwich. The children were changing classes at the time when their world was turned upside down by a blinding flash and loud explosion. Seven children were injured and taken to hospital and 21 others and a teacher were slightly hurt. A man who had been leading horses across a nearby field was badly injured by a piece of the shattered rocket which had struck him on the neck.

One of the most eventful days was Tuesday October 3 when six missiles were fired at Norfolk. At regular intervals the earth shook, windows were shattered and huge columns of black smoke mushroomed into the sky. Not one of those six found a populated area. The first arrived at Beeston St Lawrence Park, the second plunged into the sea, the third made a crater near Valley Farm, Hopton in Suffolk — from where six people were taken to hospital —the fourth hit meadowland at Witchingham, not far from Attlebridge airfield, the fifth fell onto Hellesdon Golf Course, damaging 400

On October 26, two weeks after the rocket assault on East Anglia had ended, a stray missile fell at Welborne, near Mattishall, Norfolk. The V2 caused a crater 15 feet deep by 41 feet wide and damage was caused to 15 farm buildings, a school and 15 houses. Two men were slightly hurt and a wing was broken off a passing skylark. Photograph shows the bird being examined by LAC Dunthorne (right) and a USAAF officer from Attlebridge airfield and comes to us by courtesy of P.A. Dunthorne (via Bob Collis). Bob is an aviation historian from Lowestoft.

houses — and the sixth exploded in a field at Darrow Farm, Denton, 11 miles away.

The last rocket to leave Rijs Wood for East Anglia was at 7.40 am on October 12. It fell harmlessly in open country at Manor Farm, Ingworth, causing minor damage to 24 houses. Characterising the failure of this episode of the campaign, it was to be the last V2, not intended for London, to fall on British soil.

The attacks on Ipswich and Norwich were over but the Germans did not abandon Rijs Wood. Information had reached the unit that the Belgian port of Antwerp was now in Allied hands and massive quantities of equipment for the troops were being unloaded.

Hans Klammer instructed his men to change the direction of the rockets and tilt them towards Antwerp.

The Belgian town of Antwerp was now in Allied hands and, critical to the success of the continuing advance, it was imperative to bring the port into operation as soon as possible in order to provide a shorter supply route to the front. Hitler, of course, was aware of this. On October 13, the German High Command instructed Hans Klammer to switch his emphasis from Norfolk to Antwerp and destroy it completely. Between October 13 and 20, 23 rockets were launched from Rijs towards the harbour installations. On October 21, at 4.50 pm. Batterie 444 left Rijs Wood. Some 20 minutes later seven Tempests of No 274 Squadron arrived overhead and, flying in a line astern, strafed the now-abandoned rocket base. The army, however, were well clear, having themselves blown up what was left behind. This damaged rocket, found later in the campaign by advancing commandos, shows that the retreating Nazis were leaving behind no souvenirs.

Between October 4 and 11, 62 flying bombs were launched from Heinkel 111s, of which nine fell on London. During this period 16 people were killed at Hornsey, six at Chertsey, four at Harrow and two at Surbiton. All the air launches took place during the hours of darkness and night fighters could not approach closer to the coast than six miles to seaward and five miles landward. Many Heinkels and their bombs were destroyed by fighters but it was the gunners in the new belt, northwards from Clacton to Great Yarmouth, who were again achieving the greater rate of success. The balloon barrage, too, had its moments. On October 8, a doodlebug caught in the cable crashed onto the village of Fawkham, near Gravesend, demolishing several houses. There were many casualties.

Heaven in Hellfire Corner

WITH all fears of a German invasion of Britain finally over, the Home Office made the decision to stand down the Home Guard. On Sunday October 15, more than 3,000 men and officers drawn from 50 battalions throughout Kent were among the first in the country to attend a stand-down service. The men, accompanied by bands of the 1st (Ashford) and the 18th (Dartford) fell in at the Chaucer Barracks, Canterbury and marched through the city to the Cathedral.

Lord Cornwallis, the new Lord Lieutenant of the County, took the salute outside the city walls after the service where he said: "When we in deep anguish received into our little Kentish ports our hard-pressed armies retreating from Dunkirk and when we saw endless train loads being taken back to the west through our county for rest and refitting, we might have thought there was little hope. But always remember with pride that when those tired armies were going back west, a citizens' army was rising in the south-east, ready to fight on the beaches, in the fields and in the streets to secure the breathing space the nation so urgently required. That citizen army was you — the Home Guard of Kent — and today I give to you all the humble and completely sincere thanks of the people of your country."

Three days later the now-peaceful front-line towns of Folkestone and Dover received a visit from King George V1 and Queen Elizabeth who paid their personal tribute to members of the town's Civil Defence services. After all the bombing raids, the doodlebugs, anti-aircraft guns and intensive cross-Channel shelling, there was a strange silence in Dover and Folkestone. There were no explosions and people were actually sleeping in their own beds.

Queen Elizabeth chats to members of the National Fire Service during her visit to Folkestone on October 18, 1944.

The Southend rocket is removed for examination.

Southend under fire

THE Market Garden debacle allowed Hans Klammer to send two rocket batteries back to The Hague to resume the attack on London, confident that the Allied advance from the south had been successfully halted. East London and Essex were now in the firing line and in the next few days V2s plunged to earth in Leytonstone, killing eight people, Tilbury, Wanstead and Walthamstow.

Southend was also subjected to assault by the V2; missiles fell at Pitsea and Rawreth and, on October 11 at 6.50 am, one exploded in the soft mud of the foreshore about 70 yards west of Southend Pier and left the inhabitants reflecting on what might have been, for had the V2 fallen a few yards inland the casualties would have been severe.

As it was, windows were blasted and roofs torn away from houses, shops and hotels in The Royal Terrace, Marine Parade and the High Street. Parts of the missile crashed through the Pier Pavilion and a large section embedded itself in the sea wall which surrounded the boating pool.

The incident happened at a time when there was still a total news ban on the V2, partly for morale at home but also to keep the Germans guessing. It also had the people of Southend guessing, especially those who touched the metal soon after the missile landed and found their fingers blistered and seared. The burns were due to the intense heat of the metal caused by its supersonic race through space. One white hot piece crashed through the roof of a house in Pleasant Road and fell on a bed in which 71-year-old Mrs Alice Gaylor was sleeping. The bed caught fire but Mrs Gaylor escaped with slight burns.

In the weeks that followed the people of south-east Essex became accustomed to hearing the explosions of the rockets as they bombarded the district, fortunately without any serious casualties. Damage was done at Rawreth, Wickford, Little Wakering, Fambridge, Rayleigh, Fobbing, Laindon, Canvey and many places in the Dengie Hundred and Billericay urban district.

BIG BEN INCIDENTS: SEPT/OCT 1944

This list shows the date, time and location of almost every Big Ben (V2) incident in the UK during September and October. Other months follow until the end of the rocket campaign in March

September 1944

8th (18.43) **Chiswick**
(18.43) Parndon Wood, nr **Epping**
10th (21.30) **Fambridge**, nr Southend
11th (09.07) **Lullingstone**, nr Crockenhill
(09.30) **Magdalen Laver**
12th (06.15) **Kew Gardens**
(08.19) **Dagenham**
(08.52) **Keston, nr** Biggin Hill
(17.55) **Paglesham**, nr Rochford
14th (04.53) **Walthamstow** (date corr.)
13th (11.05) Sea off **Colne Point**
14th (07.25) **Woolwich**
(13.16) **Rotherfield**
15th (04.09) **Sunbury**
(14.20) River N of **All Hallows**
16th (07.33) **Southgate**
(08.28) **Wembley**
(10.28) **Yiewsley**
(15.20) **Willingdon**, nr Eastbourne
(22.38) Noak Hill, nr **Romford**
17th (05.11) **Knockholt**
(06.04) **East Ham**
(12.05) **Hockley**, nr Southend
(13.11) **Coulsdon**
(18.56) **Brockley,** Lewisham
18th (19.02) **Lambeth**
25th (19.10) **Hoxne**
26th (16.30) **Ranworth**
27th (10.47) **Horsford**, N of Norwich
(16.25) **Kirby Bedon**, SE of Norwich
(17.50) **Beighton**, ESE Norwich
28th (14.20) 8 miles NE **Happisburgh**
29th (13.12) **Hemsby**, nr Yarmouth
(19.45) **Horstead**
(20.42) **Witlingham**, nr Norwich
30th (12.14) **Tunstall**, E of Norwich

October

1st (17.55) **Bedingham**, NW Bungay
3rd (09.32) **Beeston St Lawrence**
(14.41) **Hopton,** NW Lowestoft
(16.55) Mill Farm, **Gt Witchingham**
(19.45) **Hellesdon**
(20.10) Darrow Farm, **Denton**
(23.05) **Wanstead** (Leytonstone in original Fighter Comm. list)
4th (08.15) **Eastchurch**, Isle of Sheppey
(12.22) Sea 8 miles off **Yarmouth**
(13.40) **Rockland St Mary**, Norwich
(16.47) **Crostwick**, nr Norwich
(17.36) **Spixworth**
5th (04.22) **Goose Green**, Hoddesdon
(07.36) Sea off **Great Yarmouth**
(09.04) Taverham Hall Fm, **Norwich**
(11.38) **Peasenhall**
(13.28) **Surlingham**
(16.09) **Acle**
(17.44) **Little Plumstead**
6th (09.25) **Shotesham** All Saints
7th (08.53) **Pitsea,** nr Southend

8th (08.03) **Tilbury**
9th (05.52) **Wanstead Flats**
(09.50) **Havengore Island**
(10.45) **Langley**, SE Norwich
(10.50) **Brooke**, SE Norwich
(13.50) Hyde Marsh, nr **Fambridge**
(18.30) Sea off **Orfordness**
10th (07.19) Sea off **Clacton**
(10.25) **Navestock**, NW Brentwood
(16.00) **Harwick Harbour** (air burst)
(17.35) **Bramerton**, SE Norwich
11th (00.45) **Rawreth,** NW Southend
(05.20) North of **Ockendon**
(06.50) **Southend**
(08.10) **Haddiscoe**, nr Beccles
(10.51) **Rockland St Mary**, Norwich
(14.21) **Playford**, NE Ipswich
12th (00.12)**Walthamstow**
(02.53) Sea off **Southend**
(07.40) **Ingworth**, N of Aylsham
(10.58) **Rawreth**, NW Southend
13th (06.48) **Great Burstead**, Brentwood
(07.24) **Little Wakering**, Southend

14th (02.22) 1 mile E of Northaw
(23.50) Nr **Fairlop** airfield
15th (05.05) **Rettenden**, SE Chelmsford
17th (15.50) **Little Baddow**, Chelmsford
18th (06.32) **Chislet**, NE Canterbury
19th (07.17) **Borough Green**
20th (20.15) **South Norwood**
21st (01.15) **Hayes**
23rd (03.44) Sea 1 mile SW **Clacton**
(14.10) Felmore Farm, **Billericay**
(16.53) St Mary's at **Hoo,** Chatham
(19.18) **Navestock Heath**
24th (00.28) **Langdon Hill**, Tilbury
(02.07) Sea nr **Queenborough**
(05.02) **Rushmere St Andrew**
(20.44) **Wickford**, Essex
(20.47) **Fobbing**, Essex
(22.27) Nr **Southminster**
25th (12.40) **Rawreth**, Essex
26th (08.10) **Walthamstow**
(08.40) **Bermondsey**
(09.00) **Barley,** 3m SE of Royston

(10.14) **Welborne**, 10m W of Norwich
(11.35) **Sheering**
(13.41) Sea off **Clacton**
(18.45) **Palmers Green**
(22.50) **Ilford**
27th (06.55) nr **Slough**
(10.15) In field nr **Swanley**
(11.21) **Wanstead**
(12.05) **Chingford,** forest land
(18.54) **Wanstead**
(23.25) **West Ham**
(23.47) **Lewisham**
28th (04.59) **Ashford**, nr Staines
(11.07) **Deptford** (mid-air burst)
(18.15) **Shalford**, nr Braintree
(18.20) **Camberwell**
29th (23.57) **Shenfield**, Essex
30th (05.15) **Beckton**, nr Barking
(12.30) **West Ham**, Victoria Dock
(12.31) **West Ham**, Forest Lane
(16.23) **Woolwich**
(18.47) **Wapping**, Hermitage Wharf
(20.38) **Elstree**, Ridge Hill
31st (02.56) **Hanwell** Golf Course
(07.40) **Surrey Commercial Docks**
(18.11) **Bexleyheath**
(18.36) NE **Woolwich**
(21.03) **Hendon**, Kingsbury area
(23.40) **Orpington**

Throughout the duration of the war, the people of Dover suffered more consistent bombardment and more heartbreak than any other town in the south-east, outside of London. More than 10,000 properties were damaged, 199 people were killed and 307 seriously injured. Here are some of the survivors holding gifts sent by the people of Salford to help in "some small way to compensate their suffering". The scheme was run by the WVS.

As Canadian and British commandos, joined by Dutch and French units, advanced towards Walcheren Island where a rocket base had been established, the Germans were forced to retreat even further eastwards. Field Marshal Montgomery had an early opportunity to examine the remains of a V2 which crashed in open country near Antwerp on October 30, close to the headquarters of Major General Hobart, GOC 79th Armoured Division who is seen in the photograph.

Churchill admits: we are under attack again

ON Wednesday November 10, the Prime Minister finally admitted that Britain was under attack by the secret long-range German weapon, the V2. He told the House of Commons that almost 100 had landed since the first hit Chiswick but the information had been suppressed for very good reasons. Winston Churchill's statement followed an announcement on German radio that London "was devastated" by the weapon. The Prime Minister denied this.

"For the last few weeks the enemy has been using his new weapon, the long-range rocket, and a number have landed at widely scattered points in this country. In all, the casualties and damage have so far not been heavy, though I am sure the House will wish me to express my sympathy with the victims of this as with other attacks,

No official statement about this attack has hitherto been issued. The reason for this silence was that any announcement might have given information useful to the enemy, and we were confirmed in this course by the fact that, until two days ago, the enemy had made no mention of this weapon in his communiques. Last Wednesday an official announcement followed by a number of highly coloured accounts of attacks on this country was issued by German High Command. I do not wish to comment upon it, except to say that the statements in this announcement are a good reflection of what the German Government would wish their people to believe, and of their desperate need to afford them some encouragement.

I may however, mention a few facts. The rocket contains approximately the same quantity of explosive as the flying bomb. However, it is designed to penetrate rather deeper before exploding. The result is somewhat heavier damage in the immediate vicinity of the crater, but rather less extensive blast effect. The rocket flies through the stratosphere, going up to 60 or 70 miles, and outstrips sound. Because of its high speed. no reliable or sufficient public warning can, in present circumstances, be given. There is, however, no need to exaggerate the danger. The scale and effect of the attack have not hitherto been significant.

Some rockets have been fired at us from the island of Walcheren.

This is now in our hands, and other areas from which rockets have been or can at present be fired against this country will doubtless be overrun by our forces in due course. We cannot, however, be certain that the enemy will not be able to increase the range, either by reducing the weight of the warhead or by other methods. Nor, on the other hand, can we be certain that any new launching areas which he may establish further back will not also in turn be overrun by the advancing Allied armies.*

The use of this weapon is another attempt by the enemy to attack the morale of our civil population in the vain hope that he may somehow by this means stave off the defeat which faces him in the field. Doubtless the enemy has hoped by his announcement to induce us to give him information which he had failed to get otherwise. I am sure that this House, the Press and the public will refuse to oblige him in this respect."

Churchill spoke about the vain attempt by the enemy to attack the morale of the British people. With his process of indiscriminate slaughter and destruction, lasting for five long years, Hitler managed to kindle, in British hearts, a great fire of defiance which is brilliantly illustrated in this photograph of an old couple salvaging household goods from their bombed home — perhaps for the umpteenth time.

Carnage in Antwerp

Heavy censorship on press reports and photographs continued to apply. "Do not publish the report of the sounding of an air-raid warning in London", editors were told. "Do not publish obituary notices for people killed by enemy action." Do not publish the shooting down or the crashing of an aircraft, whether pilotless or piloted." Photographs were submitted to the censor's office before they could be used and easily-identified buildings were blacked out.
The caption of this Associated Press picture reads: Furniture and other household belongings from wrecked homes are piled in the street after a robot weapon had crashed in Southern England. Where is it ? Readers may be able to identify.

ALTHOUGH the great Belgian port of Antwerp had been on the receiving end of V1 and V2 attacks since early October, Hitler was so desperate to deny the Allies the use of the port that he ordered the attacks to be increased. This, he thought, would give him time to mount his master plan — a breakthrough in the Ardennes, cutting the Allies in two, as he had done in 1940.

For the rest of October more than 150 flying bombs and 100 rockets pounded the city, destroying many buildings and killing hundreds of people. The assault continued throughout November and, on the 27th of that month, a V2 landed on Terniers Square in the heart of the city. A military convoy was crossing a road junction at the time and 29 servicemen were among the 157 killed.

The most horrifying incident of the vengeance campaign occurred on December 16, the day the Ardennes offensives began, when a rocket landed on top of the Rex Cinema in Antwerp. The cinema was packed to capacity at the time and the carnage was terrible — 567 killed of which 296 were Allied servicemen and women.

By the end of the campaign, in March 1945, Antwerp had received 2,248 V1s and 1,712 V2s.

Thameside suffers

AFTER a relatively quiet October and a growing feeling of optimism that Kent would now be spared from any more damage, the month of November proved to be busy for the emergency services — especially in the Thameside towns. A flying bomb fell in the Grafton Avenue/Jackson Avenue area of Rochester on November 8 at 8.45 pm. More than 500 homes were damaged and the casualty detector unit was needed to help find some of the victims. Eight people were killed.

Five days later, Gravesend suffered Kent's first serious V2 incident when a missile exploded in Portland Avenue damaging the town's Co-op stores. Five were killed and 16 seriously injured. A mortar bomb hit Chatham on November 13 and towards the end of the month, Gravesend suffered a second rocket attack. This one came down in the town centre near Milton Place.

Among the eight people killed was a young serviceman who was spending his last evening on leave with his fiancée. The couple were trapped in the explosion and rescuers, including many sailors, worked for hours in the glare of floodlights to reach them. They found the man dead with his arms around his girlfriend, who was alive and conscious. He had died protecting her.

The highest V1 casualty toll in the new phase of the assault occurred at Purley in Surrey when a bomb, released from a Heinkel, dived onto the St Marie Hotel, Purley, killed 19 people and injured 30. Many guests were buried alive under the wreckage and rescue teams, with Alsatian dogs, worked all night to reach them.

This is almost certainly Grafton Avenue, Rochester on the morning of November 9, 1944, after the flying bomb attack of the previous evening. Eight people were killed and more than 500 homes damaged.

Gigantic wall of blast

FOR London, and particularly south-east London, November was also a disastrous month. It started on the first day with three V2s falling within a few miles, all causing multiple fatalities. The first hit Eglinton Road, Woolwich, killing seven people including four members of one family, the second was at Dulwich in which 24 people died and the third was at Brockley.

In his book *Bolts from the Blue*, Lewis Blake writes: *"Among the stars made pale by the moonlight a more fiery glow suddenly appeared, a man-made intruder in the firmament. It grew larger and brighter by the second, shooting earthwards at a speed almost too great for the human eye to follow. Brockley's crowded Victorian Terrace lay directly in its path, but there was no sound to warn the inhabitants of their immediate peril. A brilliant flash of light, a gigantic wall of blast, a mighty roar — in an instant the damage was done. The tram-track passing the corner of Shardeloes Road and St. Donatt's Road was blown skyhigh in a huge fountain of debris. A dozen three-up one-down dwellings sagged and tumbled to the ground like so much builder's rubble. The very earth seemed to jerk upwards and fall back."*

By dawn only 11 bodies at Brockley had been recovered; the death toll eventually reached 35 with another 155 injured. In these harrowing conditions the rescue services worked feverishly through the night and several awards for courage and devotion to duty were won.

A few days later the same rescuers were at another battlefield. On the gloomy evening of November 11 an enormous explosion filled the air from the direction of Shooters Hill; a V2 had impacted in the roadway and created a scene of utter horror. A bus with its top deck missing and the rest of the vehicle in flames was caught in the explosion and its 16 passengers never stood a chance. The Brook public house had collapsed, burying many customers, none of whom survived. The ambulance station alongside the Brook Hospital was in ruins and, in the hospital itself, there were more trapped victims. Some were located by an Alsatian search dog. Twenty six people died.

Rescue workers led by Thorn, the tail-wagging Alsatian with a habit of locating the exact whereabouts of V-bomb victims, searched among the debris for those who might still be trapped beneath the crushed wards of Brook Hospital, Woolwich.

The battlefield at New Cross

ALMOST every day throughout November there were reports of rocket incidents in the London boroughs. The Light and Heavy Rescue teams, the Express Casualty Service, ambulancemen and firemen, ARP workers, the WVS and those operating the mortuary vehicles and mobile canteens were regularly finding a huge crater in the midst of yet another devastated community. As stretcher bearers carried out the dead and Alsatian dogs helped to look for buried victims, policemen took charge of personal possessions that lay amongst the debris. Eleven died at Forest Hill, nine at Peckham, four at Welling, 31 at Deptford, 19 at Aldgate, 25 at Bethnal Green, 18 at Poplar, 24 at Greenwich, 33 at Wandsworth and 16 at Greenwich again. On top of this the Germans produced more aircraft from which to launch V1 attacks, which increased both in scale and duration. They came across the East Anglian coast and the Thames Estuary. London was under incessant fire — and the war was almost won !

By Saturday November 25 — the day on which Hans Klammer was preparing to launch his 250th rocket against England — most Londoners had grown accustomed to the sound of explosions which rolled across the sky. They frequently wondered if they would be next.

The 250th was an innocuous affair for it burst in the air over open country above Cookham Road between Sidcup and St Paul's Cray. The next one, however, was to cause Britain's worst disaster in the whole of the V-weapon campaign. The missile fell at 12.26 pm to the rear of Woolworth's in New Cross Road. The store, which was full of women and children, bulged slightly outwards and then collapsed inwards in a great cloud of dust and smoke which mushroomed high into the air. Those inside the shop stood no chance.

Next door to Woolworth's, the Co-op also disintegrated killing more people. Passers-by were lifted into the air and thrown great distances, a bus in the New Cross Road spun round like a top and then completely buckled, lorries overturned, people in offices were killed at their desks, parked cars and delivery vans burst into flames.

Lewis Blake in *Bolts from the Blue* describes the scene: *"Wrecked shops and houses stretched from New Cross Gate station to Deptford Town Hall on both sides of the road and for much of Goodwood Road. Tumbled masonry completely blocked the A2 and everywhere lay ankle deep in broken glass. A traffic hold-up in Deptford had brought a temporary lull in the usual busy stream of tramcars, otherwise the carnage would have been greater still. As it was, scores of dazed and blood-covered victims moaned on the pavements, or ran hysterically they knew not where. Others were silent and motionless."*

"Such were some of the scenes that confronted the C.D. services which rushed to New Cross from all over SE boroughs. No need to visit Europe to view a battlefield; here in an ordinary London shopping street was one as bloody as the front line could offer. The small borough of Deptford had experienced more of its share of a "people's war" since 1940, but this calamity exceeded all in its scale of suffering.

It took many days and nights to extricate the bodies of the dead and badly injured from underneath the mountain of rubble that once had been two of the most popular stores in the road. All the usual rescue services were there including many sailors from the Royal Naval College at Greenwich. Floodlights were set up and mobile cranes were brought in to lift clear the huge pieces of masonry which spilled across the road. The bodies were taken to the municipal mortuary but that was soon full and a nearby firm offered to accommodate the dead.

Officially the death toll was 160 but it was obviously higher for 11 people were missing, including two women who had gone to Woolworth's for tea with their babies in prams. They were never seen again. More than 120 people were seriously injured and an unknown number slightly injured.

The Civil Defence Controller said after the incident: "We bled the Group white for services at New Cross Road. We could not have dealt with another incident at the same time".

THE LOUDEST OF ALL

ONE of the greatest explosions in Britain during November 1944 was not caused by a V1 or V2 but a beach land mine. At 5.00 am on November 22, a barge carrying 180 tons of high explosive broke its tow during a storm in the Channel and drifted ashore to the west of Newhaven where it struck the mine. Hundreds of houses were damaged by the blast which was felt up to seven miles away. A naval rating, crushed by a falling wall, was the only person to die but many others suffered from shock and injury.

This is the scene at New Cross after Britain's worst V-bomb disaster. So great was the explosion that a delivery boy some 400 yards away felt the wave of blast warm to his face and others at a similar distance were physically pushed backwards.   This photograph shows the junction between New Cross Road and Goodwood Road.

Mr Ron Paskell of Fareham, Hampshire sent us this photograph of Christ Church, Battersea which was destroyed by a V2 rocket at 11.14 pm on November 21, 1944. He writes: "As an 11-year-old Battersea boy I knew the church well because every weekday I would stand at the bus stop facing the side of the building to catch a No 31 or No 12 tram to school. The photograph was taken by a local resident just after the bomb had fallen and is just about at the position of the tram stop. For me memories of the V1 and V2 were recalled when watching the Cruise missiles during the bombing of Baghdad during the Gulf war."

Rocket watch

IT was possible, in theory, to give London a four-minute warning of a V2 rocket launch. They came from five selected radar stations at Bawdsey and High Street in Suffolk, Great Bromley in Essex and Dunkirk and Swingate (Dover) in Kent. Here young women, who had learned to detect the "echoes" of V2s by watching cathode tubes, were on a continuous round-the-clock Big Ben rocket watch.

When the women had identified the "echoes" as coming in England's direction they would report each one to the RAF Filter Room at No 11 Group HQ who would then put the usual alert procedures into effect. It was, in the early days, a hit and miss affair because the warning was given when the rocket was still climbing and it was likely to fall anywhere, including into the sea.

Later in the campaign the problem was largely solved by a special setting of gun-laying (GL) radars located at Southwold, Aldeburgh and Walmer. When a rocket crossed these radar beams between certain limits it would indicate if it was likely to fall in the London area. The warning time was less than two minutes.

BIG BEN INCIDENTS: NOVEMBER 1944

1st (02.15) **Woolwich**
(05.13) **Dulwich**
(18.32) **Wanstead Flats**
(18.32) **Deptford**
(22.45) **Dartford**
2nd (03.30) **Ditton**
(10.05) **Lewisham**
(17.00) **Banstead**
(20.58) **Long Reach**
3rd (00.58) **Hornchurch**
(04.38) **Lewisham**
(10.45) **Barking**, Creekmouth
4th (10.56) **Ilford**
(17.25) **Sutton-at-Hone**
(18.05) Wakering Stairs, **Southend**
(21.47) N of **Romford**
5th (00.36) **Romford**
(01.30) **Penshurst**
(07.45) **Wandsworth**
(10.55) **Bermondsey**
(12.45) **Rainham**, nr Barking
(16.41) **Dagenham**
(17.12) **Islington**
6th (09.45) **Luton**
(10.51) **Yalding**, SW of Maidstone
(14.58) **Bexleyheath**
(17.50) **Little Warley**, nr Brentwood
7th (1.08) **Weeley**, nr Clacton
(09.04) **Canvey Island** area
10th (06.45) Sea off **Shoeburyness**
(08.15) **Hornsey**
(11.50) **Belvedere**
(14.51) **Middlesex Street,**
(15.10) **Fulbourne**, nr Cambridge
11th (15.40) **Cliffe-at-Hooe** (in woods)
(18.37) Shooters Hill, **Greenwich**
(19.09) S of **Birchington**, Kent
(23.44) Brook Place, **Ide Hill**, Sevenoaks
12th (00.08) Rochester Gardens, **Ilford**
(02.29) Noak Hill, NE **Romford**
(11.35) **Nazeing**, Essex
(17.30) **Stone**, nr Dartford

(20.53) **Westminster**
(21.56) **West Ham**
(23.43) **Swanscombe**
13th (04.32) **Ockendon**
(05.08) **West Ham**
(08.12) Sea, NE of **Clacton**
(12.49) **Erith**
(16.38) **Gravesend**
(22.17) Langdon Hills, **Brentwood**
(22.47) **Southborough**
14th (06.21) **Orpington**
(09.38) **Eltham**
(09.40) **Greenwich**
(21.37) **Tifford** area
(22.16) **Rayleigh**
(22.25) **Bermondsey**
15th (00.08) **Stratford**, Leytonstone Road
(02.06) **Southgate**
(05.12) **Romford**
(05.50) Between **Hertford & Harlow**
(09.19) Sea off **Southend**
(12.50) **Lewisham**
(16.43) **High Ongar**
(17.18) **Finchley**
(02.45) **Islington**
(07.40) **Collier Row**
17th (02.40) **Barking**
(03.27) North of **Dartford**
(04.50) **West Ham**
(09.15) **Poplar** (mid-air burst)
(10.56) Sea off **Clacton**
(21.45) **Rainham**
18th (11.13) **Stanford Rivers**
(11.16) **Chadwell Heath**
(11.28) **Woolwich**
(16.07) **Theydon Mount**, SE Epping
(16.08) **Erith**
(19.48) **East Ham**
(22.32) **Dagenham**
19th (02.10) **Walthamstow**
(07.05) **Peckham**
(08.31) **Wandsworth**

(10.58) **Hackney**
(16.25) Warren Hill, **Chigwell**
(19.22) **Welling**
(21.18) **Bromley**
20th (01.02) **Pinner**
(10.00) **East Ham**
(13.15) **Abridge**, nr Epping
(18.52) **Plumstead** Marshes
(20.54) **Woodford Bridge** (airburst)
21st (02.52) **Tilbury** area
(05.37) **Erith** Marshes
(12.00) **Walthamstow**
(12.03) **Little Waltham**
(13.20) **Erith**
(15.17) **Laindon**
(18.02) **Orpington**
(23.14) **Battersea**
22nd (13.27) **Bradwell** Marshes
(15.04) **All Hallows**
(16.02) **Great Wakering**
(19.40) **Bethnal Green**
(20.34) **Welling**
(21.07) **Ilford**
(23.15) **Dagenham** Marshes
23rd (01.55) **Silvertown**
(19.32) **Westwick**
(20.13) **Finsbury**
(20.15) **Bowers Gifford**
24th (03.37) **West Ham**
(08.00) **Waltham Cross**
(10.45) **Braughing**, Herts
(10.52) **Ilford**
(12.02) **West Ham**
(12.07) **Tillingham**
(20.32) **Poplar**
25th (09.25) **Wanstead**
(10.35) **Chislehurst** (mid-air burst)
(11.16) **High Holborn**
(11.30) **Great Warley**
(12.26) **Deptford**
26th (02.25) 9m SE of **Clacton**
(05.40) **Ilford**
(08.10) In sea off **Orfordness**

(11.01) **Rainham**
(11.34) **Chigwell**
(12.51) **Walthamstow**
(13.45) **Poplar**
(13.55) **Billericay**
(17.43) **Cranham**, 4m SE of Romford
(20.06) **Horndon**, 5m NE of Tilbury
(21.07) **Hertford**
(23.25) **Canvey Island**
(23.13) **Chingford**
28th (16.20) Sea 8m S of **Foulness Point**

(20.15) **Stepney** (mid-air burst)
(22.03) **East Newlands**
(23.35) **Burwash**
29th (03.13) **Barling**
(10.55) **Sandon**
(15.14) **Bradwell**
(19.50) **Polsingford**
(20.20) **Woolwich**
(21.11) **Bexley**
(23.38) **Gravesend**
(23.55) **Edmonton**
30th (00.09) **Leytonstone**
(01.10) **Greenwich**
(22.05) 2m N of **Foulness Point**

Erith in the firing line

STAFF at Erith Oil Works were leaving their canteen just after lunchtime on Tuesday November 21 when a missile exploded. Nine people caught the full force of the blast and were blown to pieces and others were stripped of their clothing. There was a thorough search for the victims over a wide area, including the roofs of the buildings.

More than 70 people were in the canteen at the time and the majority were seriously injured. A shuttle of ambulances took them away to the emergency underground hospital.

Erith received several rockets. Two fell in the Thames and, on one of these occasions, two police sergeants in their station a mile away felt earth tremors before the explosion was heard. Two also fell on the Callender Cable Works but there were no casualties. One of the worst in the borough was at Belmont Road in February 1945 when five people were killed and 62 injured.

Towards the end of November, the boroughs of Woolwich and Greenwich were under bombardment from both V1s and V2s. Six people were killed and 54 injured when a rocket fell on Green Lane, New Eltham on the 29th and 19 died when one impacted in the centre of the road at Sunfields Place, Greenwich on the 30th.

Eee, they'd a doodlebug in Oswaldtwistle !

EVERYONE said the war would be over by Christmas 1944 but, as the festive season approached, it seemed more than ever like an endless, bitter slog. The German counter offensive in the Ardennes, designed to recapture the strategically-placed port of Antwerp, was pushing back the Allies. Rockets were still pounding Greater London several times a day. The occasional air-launched doodlebug was hitting south-east England and particularly Essex. To cap a miserable year the weather was bad, with fog, drizzle and finally snow.

Only those who lived north of the Pennines felt relatively secure from the V-bomb attacks. The newspaper reports of "another tragedy in south-east England", seemed remote to the people in Lancashire, Yorkshire and Durham.

The Luftwaffe had other ideas about the North of England. In the early hours of Christmas Eve, Sunday December 24, 50 Heinkels of KG 53, each one carrying a flying bomb, crossed the coast between Skegness and Mablethorpe and released the missiles in the direction of Manchester. It was an attempt by the Nazis to outflank the east coast defences and create panic in a part of the country which had never seen a doodlebug.

Many of the missiles crashed immediately and some vanished, never to be seen again. One went down with its parent Heinkel in the North Sea and another was caught by a night fighter. The rest, 31 of them, droned on in the darkness towards the large industrial target.

Of those that went astray, one fell into the River Humber, another crashed harmlessly at Redbourne in Lincolnshire and one near Worksop. Many heard the unfamiliar sound in the sky like the rattle of a badly-tuned motorbike and evacuated London children had to explain what was happening. A teacher from Dartford in Kent was astonished when she heard a V1 during her second night in Darwen and another, which crashed near a small Lancashire village, prompted the amazed comment — "Eee, they'd a doodlebug in Oswaldtwistle".

The first to get near its target crashed, in the early morning darkness, at Hewngate Farm, Brindle, near Chorley. The Oswaldtwistle missile also crashed into farmland, close to the Haslingden to Blackburn road. A third exploded harmlessly on a golf course at Didsbury, not far from the densely populated Manchester suburb of Wythenshawe. There were casualties, however, at Davenport, near Hyde and in Worsley, where a small boy was killed.

The worst incident was at Oldham. The bomb exploded on terraced houses at the junction of Abbey Hills Road and Warren Lane where 32 people were killed and 49 badly injured. Those who died included four members of a wedding party — the bride and groom escaped — and several infants. In one house, four people were killed and five injured. Next door were three small children, evacuated from Streatham where they had already been bombed out from three homes. Their parents, Mr and Mrs Hyman, fearful of the flying bombs in London, took their little ones to "the safety" of Oldham and were actually in the house spending Christmas with them when the missile came down. Mrs Hyman was injured but the rest of the family escaped.

The only other bad incident of this raid was at Chapel Street, Tottington where seven people were killed. The missile hit a row of terraced houses, completely destroyed two of them and a shop, damaged a church and 350 other houses. Two evacuee families from London lived in one of the destroyed houses but they too escaped, having left the previous afternoon to spend Christmas in London.

The Manchester raid was notable on two counts — it provided the last serious flying bomb incident and the strangest delivery of Christmas letters ever known. Some of the missiles carried leaflets headed Vl POW post in which there were printed letters from wounded prisoners-of-war in Germany, whose homes were in the Manchester area. They were scattered about Oldham and picked up by local people who were ordered to hand them over to the police.

The letters implied the good treatment the prisoner was having and suggested that the Germans were really nice people. The intention was also to induce the addressee to write to the prisoner and disclose where the bomb had actually fallen. It was an ingenious piece of propaganda.

After the Manchester raid 60 heavy guns were moved from the east coast to the fringe Diver area between Skegness and Filey, followed by four troops of light AA guns and some searchlight detachments. The caution was understandable but KG 53 was now short of fuel and very few more V1s were fired from the air. The last one, in fact, landed at Hornsey in north-east London on January 14, 1945.

CHRISTMAS EVE IN THE NORTH OF ENGLAND

Many people in the North of England knew nothing about the flying bomb attacks on London, then suddenly they were in the thick of the action as more than 30 were scattered widely and indiscriminately across the country. The map below shows the approximate location of 28 V1s, the figure corresponding to the name of the town or village in each county.

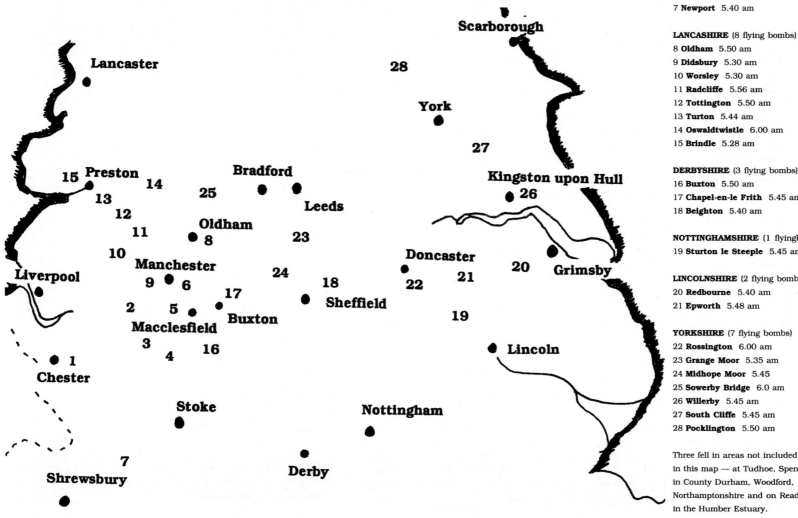

CHESHIRE (6 flying bombs)

1 **Kelsall** 6.22 am
2 **Ollerton** 6.05 am
3 **Henbury** 6.45 am
4 **Macclesfield Forest** 6.10 am
5 **Stockport** 5.30 am
6 **Hyde** 6.25 am

SHROPSHIRE (1 flying bomb)

7 **Newport** 5.40 am

LANCASHIRE (8 flying bombs)
8 **Oldham** 5.50 am
9 **Didsbury** 5.30 am
10 **Worsley** 5.30 am
11 **Radcliffe** 5.56 am
12 **Tottington** 5.50 am
13 **Turton** 5.44 am
14 **Oswaldtwistle** 6.00 am
15 **Brindle** 5.28 am

DERBYSHIRE (3 flying bombs)
16 **Buxton** 5.50 am
17 **Chapel-en-le Frith** 5.45 am
18 **Beighton** 5.40 am

NOTTINGHAMSHIRE (1 flyingbomb)
19 **Sturton le Steeple** 5.45 am

LINCOLNSHIRE (2 flying bombs)
20 **Redbourne** 5.40 am
21 **Epworth** 5.48 am

YORKSHIRE (7 flying bombs)
22 **Rossington** 6.00 am
23 **Grange Moor** 5.35 am
24 **Midhope Moor** 5.45
25 **Sowerby Bridge** 6.0 am
26 **Willerby** 5.45 am
27 **South Cliffe** 5.45 am
28 **Pocklington** 5.50 am

Three fell in areas not included in this map — at Tudhoe, Spennymoor in County Durham, Woodford, Northamptonshire and on Reads Island in the Humber Estuary.

BIG BEN INCIDENTS: DECEMBER 1944

1st(08.03)**Enfield**
(08.03)**Eltham**
(09.00)**Barking Marshes**
(09.31)**Lapwater Hall, nr Brentwood**
(10.24)**Barking**
(10.24)**Leyton**
(13.01)**Hornchurch**
(13.08)**Great Burstead**
(18.25)**Muswell Hill**
(21.12)**Paglesham, Southend**
(21.47)**Walthamstow**
2nd(07.35)**Ramsholt**
(08.20)**Sea off Clacton**
(08.31)**Benfleet**
(11.08)**Dagenham**
(20.29)**Lambeth**
(21.34)**Grays Thurrock**
3rd((06.13)**Rainham**
(07.41)**Wennington, SE of Rainham**
(09.29)**Burnham-on-Crouch**
(09.46)**Greenwich** (mid-air burst)
(10.30)**Herongate, SE Brentwood**
(12.31)**Wickford**
(14.51)In River Thames, **Erith**
(17.08)**Grays Thurrock**
(21.00)**Bexley**
4th(02.31)**Tilbury**
(09.36)**Canewdon, E of Rochford**
5th(21.38)**Dagenham**
(22.30)**Woodham Ferrers**
6th(02.31)**Great Burstead**
(02.33)**Camberwell**
(04.46)nr **Woodham Ferrers**
(05.47)25m **E of Foulness**
(07.15)**Crayford**
(10.04)15m E of **Naze**
(23.07)**Marylebone, Duke Street**
7th(01.23)**Hackney**
(02.03)**Braintree**
(20.08)**Hayes**
(03.24)**Woodford**
8th(12.45)**Canewdon**
(22.11) mile S of **Brentwood**
(23.51)E of **Tiptree**
9th(04.49)**Hornchurch**

(05.24)**Canvey Island**
(07.45)**Enfield**
(22.36)**Bowers Gifford**
10th(00.38)**Erith**
(04.50)**Lewisham**
(20.50)20m N of **North Foreland**
12th(01.21)10m SW of **Clacton**
(04.24)**Southwark**
(05.15)**Greenwich**
(06.23)**Burnham-on-Crouch**
(17.58)**Sidcup**
(20.34)**Creeksea**
(22.42)**Notting Hill**
13th(00.18)Sea SW of **Clacton**
(03.23)**Little Warley**
(07.21)**Woolwich**
(22.05)2m N of **Foulness Point**
(22.33)**Pitsea Marshes**
14th(01.09)Mouth of **River Roach**
(02.16)**Bowes Park**
(05.01)**Nuthampstead, Herts**
(17.17)**Southwark**
(20.42)4m E of **Foulness Point**
(21.06)**Great Stanbridge**
(23.39)**Highwood, nr Chelmsford**
15th(00.14)In **River Crouch,
Rayleigh**
(02.03)**High Ongar**
(02.50)9m E of **Shoeburyness**
(04.05)**Mottingham, Sidcup**
(21.48)3m E of **Clacton**
(10.43)Sea 9m SW of **Clacton**
(20.13)7m SE of **Foulness Point**
17th(16.02)**Leyton**
(18.54)**Camberwell**
18th(00.57)**Tillingham Marshes**
(16.29)**Clacton** foreshore
19th(00.47)**Hazeleigh Lodge, Maldon**
(01.25)1m N of **Chelmsford**
(06.05)**Ilford**
(11.31)**Bradwell Marshes**
(23.25)**Lewisham**
20th(02.59)**Crayford**
(12.08)**Brentwood**
(14.15)**Little Berkhamstead Hill**

(17.00)**Cuffley**
(19.20)Sea, **Foulness Point**
(20.01)**Nevendon**
21st(01.44)**Noak Hill** area
(04.34)**Brentwood**
(04.40)**Rayleigh**
(09.42)**Bradwell-on-Sea**
(10.43)**Firstead**
(16.17) **Barking**
23rd(18.49)**Bexley**
(19.40)**Hackney** (mid-air burst)
(20.28)20m E of **Shoeburyness**
(23.46)**Mildenhall** area
24th(07.37)**Wanstead**
(09.37)**Eastwood**
(23.23)4m SW of **Epping**
26th(21.05)**Nazeing**
(21.26)**Islington**
(21.45)**Pitsea**
(21.56)**Dartford Marshes**
27th(01.19)**Navestock**
(02.48)**Downham** area
(04.56)**Waltham Holy Cross**
29th(06.14)1m S of **Southminster**
(09.06)1m NE of **Mundon**
(09.16)1m NE **Burnham-on-Crouch**
(19.31)**Tillingham**
(19.54)3m E of **Brentwood**
(20.06)**Barking**
(22.38)**Croydon**
(23.20)**Shotgate, 2m E of Wickford**
30th(08.59)**West Ham**, Prince Regent Lane
(20.58)**Ilford**
(21.34)**Northfleet**
(22.34)**Sutton-at-Hone**
(22.47)**Stansgate Abbey, nr Maldon**
(22.49)**Orsett, Essex**
31st(00.35)**Ramsden Heath**
(02.09)**Enfield**
(02.55)**Rush Green, Romford**
(03.40)**Noak Hill, nr Brentwood**
(19.12)**Stow Maries, nr Maldon**
(19.46)In Sea E of **Shoeburyness**
(20.41)**Canvey Island**
(23.40)**Islington**

Boxing Day slaughter

IT was Boxing Day, 1944 and the Prince of Wales public house in Mackenzie Road, Islington had more customers than usual because the pub along the road had run out of beer and many had "transferred" before closing time. With an hour to go to closing time at 10.30 the atmosphere was noisy and convivial.

The party was abruptly and cruelly broken up by an enormous explosion. The floor of the bar collapsed and customers crashed into the cellar followed by tons of masonry. Outside a column of grey and brown smoke rose into the wintry sky. Victims, covered in blood and horribly injured but alive, tried to claw their way to safety. Someone was yelling hysterically. Others were silent and motionless.

This was the scene which greeted the rescue services in Islington on that Boxing Day evening. The rocket had exploded a few yards from the Prince of Wales in Mackenzie Road. Hundreds of houses in that heavily populated community were destroyed and the injured lay in their ruins.

One of the first on the scene was Divisional Fire Officer Cyril Demarne. "The glow of a number of fires could be seen through swirling fog as a trailer pump operator set his suction hose into an emergency water dam. He attempted to draw water without success. A horrible thought entered his mind; surely it was not empty? He shone his torch through the door and saw that the water was frozen with the suction strainer lying on the ice. He smashed the ice with a large axe and soon the water was flowing and the men were bringing the fires under control."

Throughout the night and into the next day Civil Defence rescue squads and firemen tunnelled carefully into the debris to reach those trapped in the pub cellar. One by one they lifted out the dead and injured. It was a grim and arduous task that was fraught with danger for both rescuers and victims. When the last of the bodies was recovered the next morning, the death toll had reached 68.

Unhappy New Year

THE New Year began with still no sign that the relentless pounding of London and its environs would soon end. There were hopes and there were rumours but, like a mirage, they faded. New Year V2 attacks were now averaging 10 a day and there was an increase in the number of doodlebugs. During the night of January 3/4, more than 50 V1s were launched in an attack lasting almost three hours — the longest assault since the sites were captured four months earlier. One reached London, the rest were scattered far and wide over East Anglia.

Fewer were launched on January 5 but one exploded behind the High Street in Beckenham, killing 13 people and destroying 20 houses. The next day a V2 plummeted to earth at Adolphus Road, Deptford and 20 people died. By now there were sub zero temperatures in south-east England, most of which was blanketed by heavy falls of snow. When the Deptford missile fell, burning coals from the open fires were scattered amongst the debris, setting alight many houses.

There were more tragic incidents in the suburbs — 20 killed at West Ham, 15 at Hackney, 41 at Lambeth, 29 at Islington, 14 at Rainham, Essex, 21 at Potters Bar, 12 at East Barnet, 23 at Tottenham, 30 at Southwark, 15 at Battersea and 30 again at West Ham.

The old railway tunnel at Swanscombe in Kent which led to the local lime pits, was fitted out by the local authority as an air raid shelter and was in regular use in those scary early days of 1945 when the south-east was under attack from both vengeance weapons. During the Christmas holiday, children often used to troop obediently down to the shelter and remain there for hours at a time. In January, when the new term began, the children took their chance with everyone else, for the Government was determined that schools should not close. Many argued that this was courting risk of a great tragedy; a single incident would have caused enormous public outrage. Fortunately, there were no such disasters — the closest being on December 12 when a V2 hit Morden Terrace School at 5.15 am, four hours before the children were due to assemble.

BIG BENS: JANUARY 1945

1st (01.55) **Laindon**
(04.58) **Leyton**
(05.25) **Halstead**
(06.22) **Sandon**
(08.52) **Off Foulness Point**
(20.40) **30m E of Bradwell**
2nd (03.35) **Barnes**
(09.20) **Waltham Cross**
(12.15) **Beckenham**
(15.35) **Greenwich**
(15.46) **Doddinghurst**
(18.19) **Stapleford**
(18.51) **Ramsden Heath**
(21.42) **Greenwich**
3rd (03.32) **Billericay** area
(08.39) **Edmonton**
(08.50) **Chelsea**
(13.05) **Southminster**
(18.51) **Harlow/Sheering**
(20.03) **Tonbridge**
(23.50) **Hornsey**
4th (04.19) **Hoddesdon**
(12.30) **West Ham**
(12.36) **Titsey Hill**
(12.56) **Rayleigh**
(15.43) **Runwell**
(16.13) **Hackney**
(16.13) **Little Thurrock**
(18.35) **Clothall**
(19.32) **Ilford**
(20.29) **Lambeth**
(21.06) **Stepney**
(21.21) Sea off **Southwold**
(22.54) **Dulwich**
5th (00.12) **Beckenham**
(00.43) **Navestock Side**
(03.36) **Wanstead**
(09.27) **Raydon area**
(14.12) **E of Billericay**
(15.25) **Tolleshunt D'Arcy**
(22.45) **Addington**
6th (02.15) **Dartford area**
(07.49) **SE Hatfield**
(08.32) **Ongar Park Wood**
(13.43) **Deptford**
(16.28) **Northaw**

(16.46) **West Ham**
(17.06) **Dulwich**
(19.46) **Erith**
(22.01) **Beazley End**
(22.46) **Camberwell**
7th (01.45) **Dagenham**
(02.16) **Teddington**
(04.56) **Tottenham**
(05.25) **Guildford** (Hog's Back)
(06.12) **Great Baddow**
(12.14) **Leytonstone**
(15.40) **Cheshunt**
(16.48) **Ilford**
(17.15) **Islington**
(17.36) **Hutton**
(18.13) **Brightlingsea**
8th (10.43) **High Beech**
(11.23) **Islington**
(12.13) **Sydenham**
(12.37) **Hornsey**
(13.14) **Wilmington**
(14.13) **Barking Marshes**
(15.18) **Barking**
(16.02) **Datchworth**
(16.33) **West Hampstead**
(18.22) **Clapham Common**
(19.44) **Sidcup**
(22.29) **Stoke Newington**
9th (10.50) **Beckenham**
(14.05) **South Ockendon**
(17.16) **E of Sawbridgeworth**
(18.02) **Basildon**
(19.28) **Deptford**
(22.15) **Great Warley Street**
10th (00.27) **Edmonton**
(11.00) **Great Totham**
(11.14) **Stoke Newington**
(14.20) **Henlow/Arlsley**
(14.31) **Broomfield**
11th (10.25) **Battlesbridge**
12th (11.04) **South Green**
(17.38) **Marden Ash**
(17.39) **Trimley**
(17.55) **Writtle**
(19.35) **Boreham**
(20.45) **Ilford**

(22.16) **Biddlestead**
13th (00.59) **Toot Hill**
(02.31) **Wood Green**
(06.00) **Islington**
(07.08) **Poplar**
(07.49) **Watton at Stone**
(08.57) **Broadoak End**
(11.30) **Chigwell**
(11.53) **Enfield**
(12.58) **West Ham**
(14.11) **South Hornchurch**
(16.35) **West Tilbury**
(17.58) **Hockley**
14th (10.56) **Foulness Island**
(11.35) **Abbess Roding**
(12.12) **Barking**
(13.47) **Beaumont**
(15.29) **Cheshunt**
(15.50) **Ilford**
(16.13) **Lewisham**
(17.38) **Shoreditch**
(20.59) **Barking**
15th (05.18) Off **Shoeburyness**
(09.07) **Chingford**
(11.13) **Nr Whitstable**
(17.17) **Off Polling**
(18.54) **Hackney**
(23.12) **Rainham**
16th (03.00) **Noak Hill**
(09.09) **Nr Herne Bay**
(10.59) **Chigwell**
(15.00) **Goldhanger**
(19.10) **Sidcup**
(20.32) **Cock Clarks**
(21.01) **Harlow**
(21.54) **Nr Banstead**
17th (08.18) **Mayland**
(11.42) **Bengeo**
(12.17) **Essendon**
(14.17) **Corringham Marshes**
(16.42) **East Horndon**
(16.59) **Hatfield Broad Oak**
(18.34) **Much Hadham**
(19.37) **Chingford**
19th (23.09) **Barking**

Continued on page 174

The cave dwellers

THE thousands of South Londoners who had made their home in the ancient network of caves at Chislehurst during the Blitz returned in 1944 as the rocket attacks on London increased. They were there by courtesy of the Chislehurst and Sidcup UDC's caves committee who charged 6d a week for a family "pitch". They did not have to sleep in the caves every night but lost their pitch if it were not used for three successive weeks.

At one time more than 15,000 people lived in Chislehurst caves; a small town below ground that ran with clockwork efficiency. There was water and electricity, the WVS ran canteens and supplied clothing to those who had been bombed out. There was a cinema, church, telephone kiosk, national savings bank, first aid post and shops. The committee elected marshals whose job it was to police the caves; there was a dance hall, a barber's shop and a brownie pack.

Among the distinguished visitors was Charles de Gaulle who lived for a while at 41 Birchwood Road, Petts Wood. The caves continued to be occupied up to the end of the war.

The rules of the caves (see picture) demanded that the "cave captain" control his section,, that lights must be out by 10.30 pm, that music must cease by 9 pm and that all dwellers must arrive early and "stay put". This notice survived for many years.

CHISLEHURST CAVES.

NOTICE

1 No admission or re-entry to the Dormitory Section after 9.30 p.m./or 10 p.m. during double Summer Time.
2 Shelterers already asleep in the Main Caves must not be disturbed by persons coming to their pitches.
3 Pitches must be kept clean.
4 No furniture admitted.
5 Stoves of all kinds are prohibited.
6 Rubbish must be placed in the bins.
7 Children should be on their pitches by 9 p.m. & remain there.
8 Unauthorised sale of goods is prohibited.
9 There must be reasonable quiet by 10 p.m.
10 Lights out and absolute silence by 10.30 p.m. in the Dormitory Section.
11 Pitches must not be changed, exchanged or sold.
12 Four days absence may involve loss of pitch.
13 The Cave Captain controls his section.
14 Music must cease by 9 p.m.
15 Organised concerts can be held only by permission.
16 Breach of rules involves loss of pitch.
17 Arrive early and stay put.

By Order
Caves Committee

Children queue up at the first aid post in Chislehurst caves for their weekly dose of cough medicine from Nurse Throndsen. They were not ill - the cough mixture was a substitute for sweets. The normal temperature of the caves was 48 F but this increased to 80F plus when there were 15,000 shelterers.

BIG BENS: JANUARY 1945

(continued from page 172)

(23.10) **Wanstead/Woodford**	**25th** (07.12) **Enfield**
(23.41) **Great Parndon**	(08.19) **Willesden**
20th (01.16) **Upminster**	(08.33) **Langdon Hills**
(02.57) **Canewdon**	(12.01) **Hatfield Heath**
(05.00) **Walthamstow**	(19.18) **Off Clacton**
(06.39) **East Ham**	(21.45) **Greenwich**
(08.55) **Takeley**	**26th** (06.11) **Shenley**
(10.06) **Bishop's Stortford**	(06.24) **Wanstead/Woodford**
(10.52) **Potter's Bar**	(06.32) **Woolwich**
(11.21) **Barking**	(09.05) **Leyton**
(13.15) **East Barnet**	(09.40) **Ardleigh Green, Hornchurch**
(16.09) **East Horndon**	(09.54) **Aveley**
(16.10) **Navestock**	(10.40) **Clapham**
(16.37) **Riverhead**	(12.10) **Dagenham**
(18.08) **Broxbourne**	(14.43) **Ilford**
(19.23) **Greenwich**	(18.17) **Croydon**
(19.52) **Tottenham**	(23.01) **Woolwich**
(22.49) **Wanstead/Woodford**	**27th** (00.04) **East Ham**
21st (02.05) **Plaxtol**	(02.14) **Wickford**
(12.11) **Hendon**	(03.40) **Latchingdon** area
(14.43) **Laindon**	(03.45) **East Ham**
(15.46) **Noak Hill**	(03.55) **Stanmore**
(16.50) **Greenwich**	(03.56) **Wanstead/Woodford**
(18.52) **Rainham**	(09.45) **Mountnessing**
(18.57) **Woolwich**	(12.26) **Tillingham**
(19.12) **South Ockendon**	(16.01) **Battersea**
22nd (10.12) **West Thurrock**	(16.25) **Datchworth Green**
(12.15) **Friern Barnet**	**28th** (00.19) **Forest Row**
(14.37) **Kingston-on-Thames**	(00.43) **West Ham**
(17.14) **Southwark**	(02.29) **Willesden**
23rd (08.37) **Hither Green**	(03.30) **Benenden**
(09.26) **Waltham Holy Cross**	(05.07) **Bromley**
(air burst)	(06.51) **Sidcup**
(10.50) **Mayland**	(07.30) **Kirby-le-Soken**
(11.45) **Edmonton**	(10.30) **East Ham**
(15.51) **Nr Stapleford Abbots**	**29th** (05.55) **Bradwell**
(19.14) **Dagenham**	(06.33) **Waltham Holy Cross**
(21.52) **Horton Kirby**	(07.36) **Great Amwell**
24th (09.07) **Waltham Holy Cross**	(08.52) **Darenth**
(10.50) **Enfield**	(09.22) **Shotgate**
(11.43) **Enfield**	(09.53) **Bridgemarsh Island**
(16.19) **Greenwich**	(10.02) **Stoke Newington**
(20.05) **Navestock**	(15.35) **Bradwell Bay airfield**

One of the gunners employed on the south-coast before the move to the east coast Diver Belt was Battery, later Regimental Sergeant Major Douglas Henry of 138 AA Regiment. Doug saw plenty of doodlebugs and is proud of the fact that the gunners became the first line of defence and achieved so much success. One lingering doubt still troubles him, however, and that concerns the last flight by the Band Leader Glenn Miller who took off from England on December 16, 1944 to play in Paris and went missing. It would have been a busy day for the gunners with the increased activity of air-launched V1s over East Anglia and the Thames Estuary. "Is it possible", wonders Doug, "that Glenn Miller's plane was shot down by an anti-aircraft battery?"

Brook Hospital hit again

BY the end of January, 1945 the American First Army had regained for the Allies most of the ground lost in the Ardennes, the Red Army were within 165 miles of Berlin, having established a Government of their own in Poland, Churchill and Roosevelt had met Stalin at Yalta and the flying bomb attacks on Britain had ended — for the time being. But the rockets kept coming, with many serious incidents in East London and Essex.

Communities that had already experienced the traumas of a V2 explosion were suffering again. Twenty eight were killed at West Ham, 25 at Leyton, 18 at Walthamstow, 24 at Deptford and 31 at St Pancras. It appeared those close to where a first rocket had fallen were more likely to receive another.

It was perhaps for this reason that all the patients of Brook Hospital, Woolwich, which had been badly hit by the missile of November 11, 1944, were taken to a basement shelter, leaving behind the maintenance staff on fireguard duty. It was a wise decision by the hospital authorities. In the early hours of February 20 the hospital received a direct hit and two wards were completely demolished as well as the kitchen, stores, mess room the nurses', maids' and sisters' homes, dispensary and reception rooms. Three of the fireguards were killed.

BIG BEN INCIDENTS: FEBRUARY 1945

1st (01.33) **E of North Weald**
(02.08) **Althorne**
(03.03) **West Ham**
(04.03) **Harrow**
(05.19) **Chiddingstone**
(06.11) **Walthamstow**
(07.31) **Walkern**
(07.46) **Chingford**
(10.10) **Chingford**
(14.00) **Hackney**
(14.06) **Chingford**
2nd (06.13) **Woodham Mortimer**
(08.08) **Southminster**
(08.22) **Deptford**
(10.13) **Dagenham**
(10.41) **East Ham**
(12.43) **East Ham**
(12.55) **Walthamstow**
3rd (11.25) **Epping Forest**
(13.16) **Barking**
(15.15) **Ilford**
4th (14.48) **Nr Danbury**
(15.05) **Ilford**
(15.06) **Dagenham**
(17.26) **West Ham**
(17.31) **Ilford**
(17.37) **Theydon Garnon**
(18.13) **Doddinghurst**
(18.15) **Hackney**
(22.21) **Wanstead/Woodford**
(23.51) **Nr Hornchurch**
(23.57) **Rettendon**
5th (01.59) **Chingford**
(02.39) **Hackney**
(05.35) **Epping Upland**
(08.14) **Willingale**
(09.41) **Watton-at-Stone**
(21.09) **Waltham Holy Cross**
6th (04.58) **Paglesham**
(06.38) **Essendon**
(07.34) **Tottenham**
(09.48) **St Mary Cray**
(09.51) **Ramsden Heath**
(12.56) **Bradwell Bay**
(18.05) **Crockenhill**

(19.16) **Wanstead Flats**
(21.46) **Woolwich**
7th (11.52) **Ilford**
(12.10) **Barking**
(15.59) **Waltham Holy Cross**
8th (00.32) **Bacton**
(01.08) **Walthamstow**
(02.18) **In sea, Sheringham**
(03.03) **Chislehurst**
(09.18) **Fobbing**
(10.57) **Bethnal Green**
(12.06) **Erith**
(12.35) **Ilford**
(15.43) **Rettendon**
(17.43) **Chislehurst/Sidcup**
(17.50) **Greenwich**
(20.12) **Cock Clarks**
(22.38) **Dagenham**
9th (05.42) **Navestock**
(07.26) **Stow Maries**
(14.08) **Poplar**
(16.08) **St Pancras**
(17.25) **Hayes, nr Bromley**
(19.03) **In sea south of Clacton**
(21.34) **Chislehurst**
10th (00.33) **Basildon**
(04.59) **Welling, Bexley**
(06.34) **Radley Green**
(08.28) **Leyton**
(09.24) **In sea at Bradwell**
(10.58) **Woolwich**
(11.27) **Rawreth**
(12.47) **Purleigh**
(15.03) **In sea at Clacton**
(15.29) **Margaretting**
(16.01) **Purfleet**
(19.14) **Oxted**
(20.01) **Widford**
11th (01.03) **Romford**
(01.50) **Chertsey Mead**
(04.40) **Stoke Common**
(12.31) **Stratford**
(13.31) **Bromley**
(14.51) **Walthamstow**
(16.07) **Romford**

(18.16) **East Ham**
(22.00) **Lewisham**
12th (05.15) **Leatherhead**
(07.16) **Sea off Clacton**
(07.22) **Beauchamp Roding**
(10.30) **Bayford**
(13.46) **Mountnessing**
(16.04) **Great Warley**
(18.45) **Great Totham**
(18.46) **Dengie**
(20.28) **Walthamstow**
(23.05) **Hackney**
13th (02.24) **Sea off Orfordness**
(03.42) **W of Halstead**
(06.17) **Cheshunt**
(15.49) **High Laver**
(15.53) **Thameshaven**
(16.15) **Braxted Park**
(16.33) **Erith**
(16.39) **Depden**
(16.44) **Wood Green**
(18.45) **Harold Wood**
(18.52) **West Ham**
(19.15) **Bexley**
(22.58) **Ilford**
(23.47) **Hordon-on-the-Hill**
14th (00.32) **Platt**
(02.21) **Farningham**
(03.02) **Cranham**
(05.03) **Rawreth**
(05.36) **Canvey Island**
(09.55) **Camberwell**
(14.41) **Chislehurst/Sidcup**
(14.55) **Havering**
(17.00) **Havering**
(17.11) **Finsbury**
(17.12) **Mountnessing**
(20.23) **South Green**
(21.58) **Hammersmith**
(22.31) **Hackney**
(23.57) **Latchingdon/Shoreham**
15th (00.55) **Erith**
(07.04) **Crayford**
(09.30) **Iver Heath**
(11.22) **Shoreham**

(11.36) **Corringham Marshes**
(14.47) **Sea SE of Foulness**
16th (16.10) **N of Shenfield**
(21.24) **Nr West Hanningfield**
(21.34) **West Hanningfield**
(21.54) **Woolwich**
(23.44) **Leyton**
17th (00.41) **Nr Steeple**
(00.49) **Upper Kirby**
(00.54) **Dunton**
(03.32) **Aylesford**
(03.41) **Althorne**
(04.28) **Garston Park**
(05.42) **Ilford**
(05.33) **Poplar**
(06.22) **Rawreth**
(08.10) **Lynstead**
(08.49) **Brentwood**
(11.32) **Willingale**
(14.22) **St Mary's at Hoo**
18th (00.55) **Chingford**
(01.16) **Canvey Island area**
(04.25) **Ilford**
(07.32) **Woodham Ferrers**
(08.10) **Wickford Ramsden**
(08.17) **Nr Pitsea**
(09.40) **Aveley**
(10.15) **Dartford Heath**
(12.01) **Rochester**
(12.18) **Bexley**
(14.41) **Poplar**
(15.21) **Canewdon**
(18.06) **Sea off Clacton**
(19.44) **Erith**
(19.52) **Woolwich**
19th (00.44) **Ilford**
(04.46) **Off East Anglian coast**
(04.56) **Abbess Roding**
(07.19) **Epping Forest**
(07.27) **Wanstead/Woodford**
(07.42) **Crayford**
(11.06) **Woolwich**
(11.44) **Greenwich**
(13.57) **Off Clacton**
(14.19) **Walthamstow**

(22.21) **Stoke**
(22.55) **Laindon**
20th (01.16) **Greenwich**
(04.32) **Poplar**
(08.44) **Mundon**
(09.57) **Earl Stonham**
(11.21) **Upminster**
(11.37) **Ilford**
(13.23) **Rainham**
(13.37) **Waltham Holy Cross**
(15.38) **Highwood**
(17.56) **Woolwich**
(20.35) **Romford**
(20.47) **Chingford**
(22.55) **Foulness Island**
(23.29) **Barking**
21st (09.17) **Sidcup**
(11.21) **Beckenham**
(12.58) **Ilford**
(16.17) **South Ockendon**
(22.18) **Ilford**
22nd (09.21) **Epping**
(14.46) **Eynsford**
(17.53) **Heston**
(20.11) **Sea off Clacton**
(21.02) **West Romford**
(21.48) **Althorne**
(22.48) **Warley**
(22.51) **Greenwich**
23rd (00.04) **East Ham**
(01.03) **Waltham Holy Cross**
(04.37) **Chigwell**
(07.46) **Dagenham**
(09.08) **Chigwell**
(09.45) **Sevenoaks**
(11.24) **Cheshunt**
(12.42) **Sea off Folkestone**
(13.39) **1m NW of Epping**
(14.25) **Blackmore**
(16.43) **Cold Norton**
(16.59) **Chelmsford**
24th (07.40) **Dagenham**
26th (09.10) **Woolwich**
(09.11) **Bobbingworth**
(09.35) **Ilford**
(11.27) **Belvedere, Erith**
(18.26) **Leyton**
(20.25) **West Ham**
(23.05) **Pitsea Marshes**

Crisis for Germany but the rockets keep coming

MARCH, 1945 was the crisis month for the Germans, but who in south and east of England would have believed it. Unremitting fire came from the rocket batteries in The Hague. Flying bombs reappeared after a gap of several weeks. Attacks by manned aircraft were carried out on the heaviest scale since D Day. Machine gunning, cannon fire, heavy explosives and incendiaries were all reported and in the first week of March alone civilian fatalities from all causes totalled 169.

Bomber Command was retaliating with a series of heavy raids on German cities, designed to force the Nazis to capitulate. The Russians were advancing in the east, but most of Holland was still in German hands and Col Wachtel, despite his dwindling command, was now equipped with the longer range flying bomb. New ground-launch ramps were built in The Hague and more than 100 set course for London. General Pile's men on the east coast defences, helped by the new radar techniques, were now red-hot shots and the guns accounted for 86 of the 125 which approached Britain.

There was nothing the gunners could do about the rockets. Even the more enlightened thought that was an impossible problem for AA Command. Pile and his men had other ideas. They produced a scheme, entailing the use of special radar stations to detect rockets at a height of more than 30,000 feet, predict the point of fall and burst shells in their path. The guns would have to be fired when the rockets were still 30 miles from London.

General Pile wrote: "It was variously estimated that we could blow up in the air between three and 10 per cent of all the V2s we fired at. However, Monty beat us to it and before we could wring permission out of the War Cabinet to try our plan, the rocket area of Holland was cut off by the liberation armies."

Before that happened the rockets hit London so frequently that at least one incident was reported every day of the month, up to March 27. Inevitably one hit West Ham where 31 people died. There were 52 killed at Deptford, 25 at Poplar, 23 at Leyton and 33 at Heston.

At Stepney a rocket hit Hughes Mansions and demolished two five-storey blocks of flats. The rescue teams spent hours extracting the bodies from underneath a mountain of rubble and, when they completed their gruesome task, the death toll was approaching 100. It rose eventually to 131 killed and 40 seriously injured.

This was the second biggest disaster of the entire V-weapon campaign.

Some people claim to have seen, on a clear day in a cloudless sky, a V2 rocket in its descent. It was an unusual sighting for it was visible for only four seconds during its rapid dive from about 20,000 feet, and it was far more usual for the vapour trail to be seen. This remained in the sky for up to 30 seconds. The first thing the majority of people knew about the V2 was the explosion itself, followed by another boom and then the descending whistle indicating that the rocket had broken the sound barrier. The picture above shows the damage caused by a V2 which crashed at Limehouse in March. In the foreground a missile expert examines the propulsion unit.

Two rockets fell in the Earlham Grove area of Forest Gate in the beleagured Borough of West Ham, one on October 30, 1944 and the second on Tuesday March 6, 1945. The impact point of the second rocket can be clearly seen.

BIG BENS
FEB 1945

(continued P175)

27th (01.23) **West Thurrock Marshes**
(01.25) **Dagenham**
(02.24) **Kelvedon Hatch**
(02.29) **Ilford**
(04.43) **Chevening**
(05.33) **Theydon Garnon**
(07.45) **North Stifford**
(09.21) **Swanscombe**
(10.51) **Ingatestone**
28th (00.22) **New Hall Green**
(01.21) **Enfield**
(03.14) **East Ham**
(05.07) **Erith**

Part of the activity in Highbridge Street, Waltham Abbey where a V2, had impacted. Ted Carter and his colleagues worked non-stop for 30 hours, searching for bodies, pulling down dangerous buildings and bulldozing away the rubble.
In the background is Waltham Abbey, burial place of King Harold, slain by an earlier foe. With the main road through the town closed, Ted had to drive 10 miles to get his car back to the depot. "Perhaps", he said, "someone will wake up now to the sore necessity of a by-pass."

Crater in town centre

FROM the diary of Ted Carter, Chief Warden of Waltham Holy Cross, come these extracts about the rocket which caused a huge crater right across the town's one and only main road and sucked in part of the Drill Hall, several houses and a wardens' post.

Wednesday March 7: So terrific had been the flow of water from the broken mains that the crater, itself 75 ft in diameter and probably at least half that in depth, was flooded to a level above that of the adjoining road. Across the crater the whole front of the Home Guard Drill Hall had collapsed in a heap of bricks and girders. The two larger houses were only open shells, with doors, ceilings, windows and frames, stairways smashed into rubble.

Our new control room was out of action and all telephone lines westward were gone completely, and shadow control in the Abbey crypt had to function as best as it could. The NFS ran out emergency field telephones to link up Control Centre.

The bodies of two children had been found, and I watched the searcher dog looking for a third. With its trainer it sat crouched and tense on a heap of rubble, and giving it an encouraging pat the trainer led it off, and work started again.

As we searched I half dreaded finding anything, but when we did, it wasn't as bad as I had expected. First there was a leg. with the foot complete and uninjured but the larger bones toward the knee showing horribly between the mangled flesh. A moment or two later, another foot was found, with the shoe completely missing. The third child's body was recovered, making the total of deaths four, and injured 53.

With the dawn of the next morning, the incident came to life again; repair gangs came in from every direction, naval working parties arrived in charabancs, until Highbridge Street was busier than it had ever been before in all its long history, and cars and lorries jostled and bumped each other as they came and went.

The last rocket to cause great loss of life in Central London, dived directly onto the centre of Smithfield Market on Thursday morning March 8, at a time when the market was packed with traders and customers. It penetrated the floor and exploded in the underground railway network beneath. The buildings collapsed into the crater and the shops which had a frontage onto Farringdon Road were completely levelled. Many people dropped into the crater as the floor of Smithfield gave way and others, on the pavement outside the building, were buried by the rubble which rained down on them several seconds later. The death toll was even greater than the Boxing Day blast at Mackenzie Road — 110 people killed and many more severely injured.

Six rockets landed within a quarter-mile radius of this spot in the Wanstead Park area of Ilford. The sixth struck on Thursday March 8 between Endsleigh Gardens and Kensington Gardens, damaging most of the homes in this aerial photograph. Nine people were killed and 15 seriously injured.

BIG BEN INCIDENTS: MARCH 1945

1st (01.08) **Billericay**
(02.34) **Little Leighs**
(05.07) **Barnet**
(05.09) **Stapleford Tawney**
(05.46) **Woolwich**
(08.06) **Shoreditch**
(08.23) **Orpington**
(15.27) **Walthamstow**
(16.10) **Wickford**
(17.28) **Horndon-on-the-Hill**
(23.13) **West Ham**
2nd (01.02) **Ashington**
(02.19) **Havering**
(04.49) **Greenwich**
(04.52) **Orpington**
(05.41) **Chigwell**
(05.48) **Chigwell**
(05.51) **1m N of N Fambridge**
(07.39) **Herongate**
(07.50) **Egypt Bay**
(08.18) **Sea off Southend**
(09.22) **Brentwood**
(11.06) **Greenwich**
(12.21) **Orpington**
(23.03) **Chigwell**
(23.11) **Bermondsey**
(23.15) **Woking**
3rd (01.14) **Foulness Island**
(02.32) **Edmonton**
(03.35) **Theydon Bois**
(03.47) **Woolwich** (air burst)
(04.39) **Woolwich** (air burst)
(04.49) **Sevenoaks**
(06.01) **Ilford**
(06.14) **Sea off Clacton**
(12.17) **Deptford**
4th (01.35) **Havering-atte-Bower**
(04.52) **Penshurst**
(05.38) **Bermondsey** (air burst)
(08.20) **Chingford**
(09.08) Mouth of the Thames
5th (20.07) **Woolwich**
(22.32) **Rainham**
6th (00.57) **Bexley**
(03.07) **Rainham**

(03.09) **West Ham**
(04.35) **Sidcup**
(06.18) **Barking**
(08.35) **Woolwich**
(12.33) **Bowers Marshes**
(12.57) **Wandsworth**
(16.58) **Walthamstow**
(19.38) **Wandsworth**
(19.38) **West Ham**
(21.44) **Woolwich**
(23.24) **Ilford**
(23.26) **Chigwell**
7th (01.59) **Nr Navestock**
(03.13) **Stanford Rivers**
(03.20) **Deptford**
(06.03) **Edmonton**
(08.37) **Greenwich**
(10.33) **Sidcup area**
(12.57) **Poplar**
(14.55) **Brundish (Norfolk)**
(17.00) **Waltham Holy Cross**
(21.59) **Ilford**
(23.32) **Dagenham**
8th (00.49) **Chigwell**
(01.37) **Woolwich**
(03.24) **Writtle**
(04.21) 12m ESE of **Clacton**
(04.36) **St Mary Cray**
(05.04) **Ilford**
(09.12) **West Ham**
(11.02) **Finsbury**
(11.10) **Farringdon Road**
(12.06) **Blackheath**
(14.55) **Sidcup**
(19.53) **Horton Kirby**
(20.17) **Dunton**
(21.46) **Bennington**
(21.51) **Harold Park**
(23.03) Sea off **Canvey Island**
9th (00.40) **Kenton**
(02.18) **Marden**
(04.06) **Pitsea**
(04.27) **Greenwich**
(08.29) **Greenwich**
(08.38) Sea 3m SSW of **Southend**

(11.06) **In Thames**
(13.51) **Waltham Holy Cross**
(22.59) **South Ockendon**
10th (00.01) **Beckenham**
(00.16) **Biggin Hill**
(01.26) **Pilgrims Hatch**
(01.50) **Enfield**
(04.22) **1m SSW of Rawreth**
(09.57) **West Mill**
(10.01) **Bexley**
11th (07.09) **Nr mouth of River Crouch**
(07.40) **West Ham**
(10.02) **Westerham**
(20.04) **Deptford**
(20.40) **Canvey Island**
(21.51) **Bulphan**
12th (00.11) **Ilford**
(00.26) **Upminster**
(01.29) **Greenstead**
(02.05) Sea 6-7m SE of **Clacton**
(02.33) **Sidcup**
(02.40) **Sidcup**
(04.45) **Little Warley**
(04.47) **Hainault Forest**
(05.05) NW of **Hornchurch**
(07.01) **Woolwich**
(07.18) **Althorne**
(09.03) **Thames Estuary**
(11.17) **Lower Kirby**
(21.19) **Epping**
(23.46) **Nazeing**
13th (03.27) **Tillingham Marshes**
(06.29) **1.75m NE of Brentwood**
(08.30) **Erith**
14th (00.30) **Havering**
(21.22) **Rainham**
(23.27) **Sutton-at-Hone**
15th (00.16) In Thames at **Dagenham**
(03.33) In Thames at **Woolwich**
(06.24) **Rayleigh**
(09.11) **Richmond**
(13.27) **Tottenham**
(22.26) **Hornchurch**
(22.57) **Neasden**

(23.45) **Nr Maldon**
16th (02.34) **Willesden**
(02.54) Sea off **North Foreland**
(06.34) **Leyton**
(06.51) **Stock**
(08.53) **East Ham**
(09.37) **Dengie**
(23.06) **Basildon**
17th (00.09) 3m S of **Upminster**
(00.55) **Nr Hornchurch**
(03.34) **Wennington Marshes**
(05.16) **Hampstead**
(07.36) **Dartford**
(08.11) **Woolwich**
(12.45) **Greenwich**
(13.20) **Stepney**
(22.26) **Barking**
18th (00.38) **West Ham**
(01.33) **Cranham**
(01.41) **Battlesbridge**
(02.03) **Epping**
(03.40) **Ightham**
(06.30) **Aylesford**
(06.40) **Hutton**
(06.46) **Barking**
(09.34) **Marble Arch**
19th (00.04) **Theydon Garnon**
(00.06) 2m S of **Harlow**
(01.33) **South Hornchurch**
(01.37) **Nutfield**
(10.08) **Wargrave**
(10.31) **Erith**
(15.55) **Woolwich**
(22.20) **Theydon Bois**
(22.45) **Hatfield Broad Oak**
20th (01.28) **Little Warley**
(04.10) **West Hanningfield**
(05.37) **Hornchurch**
(07.03) **Parslow Common**
(08.20) **Sidcup**
(09.53) **Mayland**
21st (00.40) **Wanstead/Woodford**
(09.36) **Heston and Isleworth**
(11.39) **Hampstead**
(13.43) **Ruislip**

(18.44) **NE Romford**
(21.33) **6m NW Braintree**
(22.40) **Woodham Ferrers**
(23.55) 4m E **Bishops Stortford**
22nd (02.06) **Off Blackwater River**
(02.36) **Nr Canewdon**
(02.43) **Epping, Fairfield**
(03.35) **Harrow**
(03.57) **Hoo, Nr Strood**
(05.22) **Stock**
(05.47) **Boreham**, NNE Chelmsford
(06.02) **Leyton**
(07.02) **Brightlingsea**
(07.44) Sea 5m off **Bradwell**
(08.13) **Dagenham**
(09.52) **South Woodham**
(10.30) **Dagenham**
(21.45) 20m SE **Yarmouth**
(23.21) **Dartford**
(23.42) **Southminster**
23rd (01.40) **Greenwich**
(03.15) Sea off **Clacton**
(04.30) **Stepney**
(06.26) **North Weald**
(06.49) **Little Gaddesden**
(09.41) W of **Althorne**
(12.32) **Stapleford**
(23.16) **Waltham Holy Cross**
24th (01.31) **Poplar**
25th (22.33) **St Pancras**
(23.00) **Enfield**
(23.44) **Stepney**
26th (00.05) **Lambourne**
(04.04) **Cheshunt**
(04.20) **Bermondsey**
(04.42) **Hornchurch**
(09.03) **Navestock**
(14.43) **Ilford**
(15.22) **Bromley**
(19.08) **Romford**
(22.30) **Noak Hill**
27th (00.22) **Edmonton**
(03.02) **Cheshunt**
(03.30) **Ilford**
(04.04) **Hutton Park**
(07.21) **Stepney**
(16.54) **Orpington**

Final rocket falls in Orpington

IVY MILDRED MILLICHAMP
BELOVED WIFE OF ERIC
27TH MARCH 1945 AGE 34

THE LAST PERSON IN BRITAIN
TO BE KILLED BY ENEMY ACTION
ALWAYS IN OUR HEARTS
REMEMBERED WITH LOVE

TIME was running out for Hitler and for his rocket troops in The Hague. On Wednesday March 21, the Western Allies advanced across the Rhine and SS Gruppenführer Klammler was virtually cornered. He had time for a few parting shots before moving his men out of Holland, placing Britain beyond range of the V2. Before they packed their bags and left, on the afternoon of Tuesday March 27, they launched two final rockets — one to Antwerp, which killed 27 people — and one to England.

It landed at Orpington, 15 miles from the centre of London, between Court Road, part of the Orpington by-pass, and Kynaston Road gouging a hole 40 feet across and 20 feet deep in the gardens which separated the two roads. People for miles around heard the explosion. Buildings shook, windows shattered, pavements shuddered and many dived instinctively for cover.

In Kynaston Road, two small boys who had gone into the Anderson shelter at No 96 were saved from certain death. A married couple in their garden at No 84 were injured. Two old age pensioners at No 86 were more seriously hurt, as were the elderly occupants of No 82, whose roof was lifted off in the blast.

In Court Road, the owner of No 63 was shopping at the time in Petts Wood and heard the explosion. She returned to find her home gone. A police inspector at No 69 was listening to a radio programme about the war being over when the house fell on top of him. He survived.

On that spring afternoon 23 people from Kynaston Road and Court Road were seriously injured and one woman was killed. Mrs Ivy Millichamp, aged 34 of No 88 Kynaston Road, was in her kitchen when the rocket fell. She was pulled clear of the wreckage by her husband Eric but she had caught the full force of the blast and was already dead.

Ivy Millichamp was the last civilian in Britain to be killed by enemy action. She was the daughter of Mr and Mrs Benjamin Croughton who raised their large family of seven daughters and five sons in Tottenham before moving to Rayleigh in Essex. Ivy, the eighth born, married Eric Millichamp in 1938 when she was 27 and went to live in a small bungalow at Kynaston Road which was convenient for Eric's employment as an engineer.

In January, 1945 a flying bomb landed in Court Road, killing eight people but Ivy and Eric escaped unharmed. Then, just over two months later came the rocket, and Ivy suffered the cruel fate of being the last civilian to die in Britain after a long, bitter battle. She was laid to rest in All Saints Churchyard on April 3. The grave was never marked and the death certificate gave her address as No 86 Court Road but, thanks to the editor and authors of the book *"The Blitz — Then and Now — Volume Three"* the certificate was corrected. They also arranged for a suitable headstone to be erected and, on Remembrance Sunday, 1989 a memorial service was held.

The gardens behind No 88 Kynaston Road, Orpington where the final V2 rocket fell killing Mrs Ivy Millichamp.

While the Americans were transporting rockets from the underground caves at Nordhausen to Antwerp, the Germans were attempting to salvage a few V2s from other sites. At Oyle, on April 16, 1945, a trainload was shot up by the RAF while being carried on the railway. Most of the train was badly smashed and rockets destroyed but this one, almost complete, was undamaged.

The Eagle has landed

EVEN as the Third Reich faced extinction, von Braun and Dornberger were still actively engaged in their work at Peenemunde; in fact they were working on a new project, the A4b, a standard V2 modified to permit the attachment of supersonic wings. But the game was nearly up, and the rocket men realised it. They met secretly with their senior staff to decide whether to remain at Peenemunde and surrender to the Russians or move to an area likely to be occupied by the US Army.

They decided that the American option was the lesser of two evils and, ignoring orders from their Nazi bosses, von Braun, Dornberger and 4,000 employees and their families packed up large quantities of drawings and documents and headed south. Avoiding the Gestapo and the SS they finally reached the town of Bleicherode in the Harz Mountains and set about continuing with their research work.

In early April, the two men and 500 other scientists and technicians moved into Bavaria and waited in villages around the town of Oberammergau for the arrival of the Americans. They surrendered to a unit of the 44th Infantry Division on May 2, 1945 and asked if they could go to America and continue their work in rocket development there.

The Americans realised that this was an extraordinary coup. Von Braun was the outstanding spirit in the entire rocket project and his scientists had invaluable experience in rocketry and its development. About 500 of the former Peenemunde team were offered contracts to go to America. The majority accepted and there they worked happily with their old adversaries.

The great dream eventually came true. On July 20, 1969, Professor Dr Werner von Braun, as director of the Apollo Space Project, heard these historic words from Commander Neil Armstrong — "Houston. Tranquility Base here. The Eagle has landed."

Wachtel also surrenders

Colonel Wachtel of Flakregiment 155 (W) also surrendered. Driven from Holland, he retreated to Luneberg in north-west Germany and reformed his troops into infantry to fight the advancing British on the ground. On May 4, 1945, along with other German forces, he surrendered unconditionally to Field Marshal Montgomery.

Like the rocket men, the men of Flakregiment 155 (W) were not tried as war criminals and Colonel Wachtel, at the end of hostilities, secured a post in a different kind of aviation as the manager of Hamburg airport.

Dr Werner von Braun, with a broken arm, at the moment he surrendered to the troops of the 44th Division of the US Army. With him are (left) Major General Walter Dornberger, commandant of Peenemunde and (hatless) Lt. Col. Herbert Axter, senior scientist.

Throughout the V weapon campaign, the county of Kent was in the front line and became known as Hellfire Corner. 1,444 flying bombs and 67 rockets fell in Kent, and now it was all over. God bless our boys, says the banner in this street in Canterbury, where the lady on the accordion led the procession on VE Day.

Back from the jaws of death

THE Battle of the Flying Bombs was over. The German retreat became a rout. President Roosevelt died on April 12 and the next day the concentration camps at Belsen and Buchenwald were taken by the British. The Russian noose tightened around Berlin. Mussolini was executed on April 28. The survivors of Dachau death camp were liberated. On Sunday April 30, Adolf Hitler and Eva Braun, his bride of 36 hours, committed suicide in their Berlin bunker. The war was almost over.

The cost of the V weapon campaign could now be counted — 8,958 dead and 24,504 injured, a total that could well have been higher if the V3 had ever been put to use. This was a gigantic long range gun capable of firing rocket shells against London. A battery of these guns were discovered by the advancing forces in a great concrete structure at Mimoyecques, Pas de Calais. By then it had been heavily bombed and could probably have never come into action but it contained 50 smooth bore barrels approximately six inches in diameter and 416 feet long which would have fired finned projectiles, each weighing 300 pounds at a combined rate of up to 10 a minute at London.

The War Office felt that British Intelligence should have known about it, but thanks to Bomber Command the third "miracle weapon" was never more than a Nazi dream.

On Tuesday May 8 at 3pm Winston Churchill told the nation on the BBC that representatives of the German High Command had signed the act of unconditional surrender. Hostilities were to end officially at one minute after midnight.

There were wild celebrations but, coming so soon after the end of the V for Vengeance campaign, the news in many homes was greeted in a more sober fashion. These included the many families either bereaved by the bombs, or whose members bore the scars of terrible injury. They included members of the Civil Defence who had seen at first hand the hideous nature of warfare. They included the fighter and the bomber pilots who lost more than 2,900 colleagues in the V weapon battle. And they included those who mourned the loss of loved homes and prized possessions.

On Tuesday May 8, 1945, Churchill said: "The lights went out and the bombs came down. But every man, woman and child in the country had no thought of quitting the struggle. London can take it. So we came back after long months from the jaws of death, out of the mouth of hell, while all the world wondered. When shall the reputation and faith of this generation of English men and women fail ? I say that in the long years to come not only will the people of this island, but of the world, wherever the bird of freedom chirps in human hearts, look back to what we've done and they will say 'do not despair, do not yield to violence and tyranny, march straight forward and die if need be — unconquered'. Now we have emerged from one deadly struggle — a terrible foe has been cast on the ground and awaits our judgement and our mercy".

Frank Wootton's painting shows a Mustang of 170 Squadron 35 Wing PRU on aerial reconnaissance duty over a "ski" site in northern France. Photographs taken by Mustang and Mosquito pilots in November 1943 revealed construction sites with numerous small buildings of identical design on each site, including concrete platforms with a central axis bearing on London. Each site contained sheds shaped like skies on their sides. By the end of that year, 83 "ski" sites had been detected and bombers had released 3.210 tons of bombs over them.

The whole weight of Bomber Command was brought to bear against Peenemunde on the moonlit night of August 17, 1943. 596 bombers of 54 Squadrons set off across the North Sea in a bid to destroy the workshops and laboratories where the V2 was being designed and manufactured. Hundreds of airmen went on the raid. Many didn't return and many more died in subsequent bombing missions. Some 49 years later, at RAF Hendon, members of the Bomber Command Association, met for their regular summer get-together. Peenemunde was on the menu, as it always is, and here are some of the survivors representing, for the purpose of this book, the hundreds of brave men who took part in Operation Hydra, one of greatest bombing raids in history. Left to right: Warrant Officer Jack Slaughter DFM, navigator with Pathfinder Force 83 Squadron; Squadron Leader 'Pil' Pilgrim DFC FCA. pilot with 44 Squadron; Flight Lieutenant James Chapman DFC, Rear Gunner with 61 Squadron; Flight Lieutenant John Wilkin DFM, Navigator with Pathfinder Force 156 Squadron (John was one of the deputy master bombers to Squadron Leader John Searby); Flight Lieutenant Dave Francis DFC, Navigator with 460 Squadron. In the background is the bomb bay of Avro Lancaster R5868 which served with Squadrons 83 and 467. During the war this Lancaster flew on more than 120 confirmed bombing sorties. The Lancaster bomber is, of course, immortalised as the aircraft used in the attacks on the Mohner and Eder dams.

Miss Constance Babington Smith, photographed in 1992 at her home in Cambridge. Miss Babington Smith was the young WAAF officer who first identified a flying bomb at Peenemunde from a mass of photographs which she had been interpreting. She went on to enjoy a distinguished career as editorial researcher with Life Magazine and then as an author of several books including Evidence in Camera, the story of the photographic interpretation unit at Medmenham in Buckinghamshire. Her fascination for aviation has never diminished. She has written a History of British Test Flying and a full biography of Amy Johnson. Miss Babington Smith has edited the letters of Rose McAulay and, more recently, completed her latest book, Champion of Homeopathy. She has lived in Cambridge for more than 20 years.

As Military Adviser to Duncan Sandys, Colonel Kenneth Post was, from the start concerned with the battle of the flying bombs and rockets and, in 1992 when this photograph was taken at his home in Tunbridge Wells, he recalled, with great clarity, the Crossbow Committee, meetings of the War Cabinet and the often heated discussions on the prospects of the country being bombarded by Hitler's secret weapons. Colonel Post was closely involved with the decisions to bomb Peenemunde, the "ski sites" and the huge concrete works at Watten and, when the V1s began to arrive he, and others, advised Mr Sandys and the Prime Minister to move the guns to the coast out of the way of the fighters and away from the elevated North Downs. Colonel Post said: "Duncan Sandys was, in effect, heading up the whole of these operations — Bomber Command, Fighter Command, Balloon Command and the Intelligence Service. I was privileged to work alongside him and this was, by far, the most important thing I did in my life."

Mr Edwin Woods, who lived at Rhodes Minnis, near Lyminge in Kent when this photograph was taken, in 1992 was a member of the Royal Observer Corps in 1944. He was on duty at Post Mike Three when he saw a "fighter on fire" heading towards the Kent coast from Boulogne. He gave a reading to Maidstone ROC, and handed over to his colleagues at Dymchurch, unaware that he had made the first sighting of a flying bomb. He then heard the code word "diver, diver" being called for the first time. (See page 28).

Henryk Pawelec with the badge of his Polish underground unit. As commander of a resistance unit, Henryk played a vital role in unveiling the secrets of the V2 rocket and supplying priceless information to the Allies, regardless of torture and death. When this photograph was taken in 1992, Henryk and his wife ran a guest house in the Kentish town of Deal. (See page 141.)

TOP V1 SCORERS IN THE FIGHTER SQUADRONS

Number	Squadron	Aircraft	Base	Score
1:	3	Tempest 5	Newchurch/ Matlask	357
2:	486	Tempest 5	Newchurch	223
3:	91	Spitfire 14	Deanland	185
4:	96	Mosquito 13	Ford	174
5:	322	Spitfire 14	West Malling/ Deanland	108
6:	418	Mosquito 6	Holmesby/Hurn/ Middle Wallop	90
7:	129	Mustang 3	Brenzett	66

V WEAPON CASUALTIES IN EUROPE

The V Weapon casualties in Europe were as follows.

	Antwerp	Brussels	Liege	Others
Military killed	743	7	92	114
Military wounded	1,078	38	336	457
Total	1,812	45	428	571
Civilians killed	2,900	40	221	575
Civilians injured	5,433	153	937	1,643
Total	8,333	193	1,158	2,218
Grand Total	10,145	238	1,586	2,771

Other Continental centres bombed were Remagen, Arras, Cambrai, Diest, Hasselt, Lille, Maastricht, Mons, Paris, Tourcoing and Tournai

Bibliography

In writing this book I have referred to a variety of pamphlets, newspaper articles, documents and official files in the Public Record Office. Much of the information comes from members of the public who so generously responded to my appeal in local newspapers for photographs and anecdotes about the Vengeance weapon campaign. I am grateful to the archivists of various county record offices and to librarians and museum staff who showed me miscellaneous documents, war diaries, ARP reports, letters and diaries. I have also used a number of published and unpublished books.

After The Battle, *The Peenemunde Rocket Centre*, Battle of Britain Prints International
Lewis Blake, *Bromley in the Front Line*
Lewis Blake, *Bolts From the Blue*
The Blitz Then and Now, Volume Three, Battle of Britain Prints International
Bohdan Arct, *Poles against V-Weapons*, Interpress Publications, Warsaw
Constance Babington Smith, *Evidence in Camera*, Chatto and Windus.
Roland Beamont, *My Part of the Sky*, Patrick Stephens Ltd
Croydon Advertiser Ltd, *Croydon Courageous*
Winston S. Churchill, *The Second World War*, Cassell.
Peter G. Cooksley, *Flying Bomb*, Robert Hale Ltd
Joachim Engelmann, *Dawn of the Rocket Age*, Schiffer Military History
Harry Klopper, *History of Fire Fighting in Kent*, Whitefriars Press, Tonbridge
James Farrar, *The Unreturned Spring*, Chatto and Windus
Folkestone and Hythe Herald, *Front Line Folkestone*
Roy Humphreys, *Target Folkestone*, Meresborough Books, Rainham
George Humphrey, *Wartime Eastbourne*, Becket Features Ltd
Charles Graves, *Women in Green*, Heinemann
Hastings and St. Leonards Observer, *Hastings in the Front Line*
David Irving, *The Mares Nest*, Corgi Books
R.V. Jones, *Most Secret War*, Hamish Hamilton
Marcel Julian, *Jean Maridor, Chasseur de V1*, Amiot-Dumont, Paris
Judy Lomax, The Hanna Reitsch Story
Norman Longmate, *The Doodlebugs, The Story of the Flying-Bombs*, Hutchinson
Rudolf Lusar, *German Secret Weapons*, Neville Spearman
E.S.Oak-Rhind, *In Bomb Alley, the Land Girls Wept*, Local Government Service, vol XX111, no 10
General Sir Frederick Pile, *Ack-Ack*, Harrap
H.R.Pratt Boorman, *Kent Unconquered*, Kent Messenger
Andrew Rootes, *Front Line County*, Robert Hale Ltd
Sussex Express and County Herald, *War in East Sussex*
City of Westminster, *War in Westminster*

A special thank you to Mrs Avril Oswald, Miss Constance Babington Smith, Wing Commander Roland Beamont and Colonel Kenneth Post for their help in checking the manuscript.

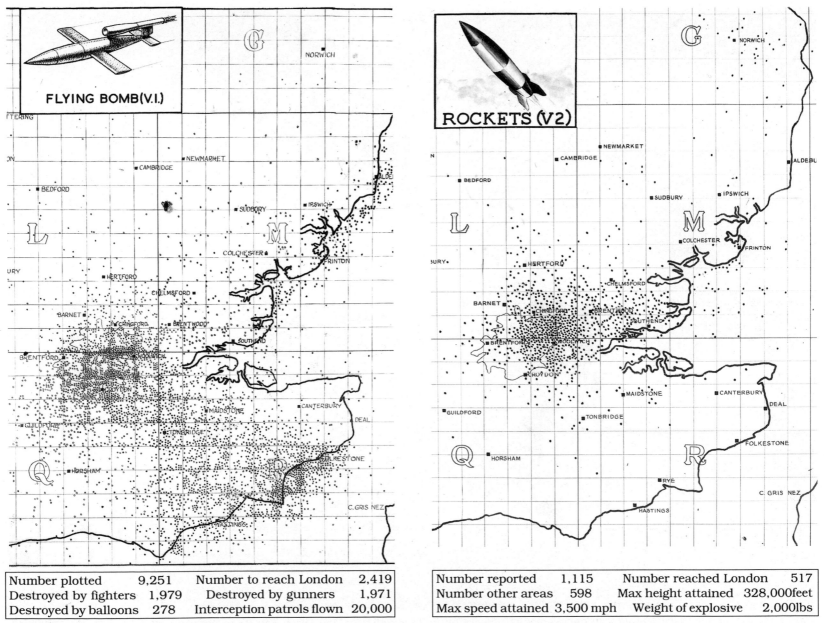

FLYING BOMB (V.I.)

ROCKETS (V2)

Number plotted	9,251	Number to reach London	2,419
Destroyed by fighters	1,979	Destroyed by gunners	1,971
Destroyed by balloons	278	Interception patrols flown	20,000

Number reported	1,115	Number reached London	517
Number other areas	598	Max height attained	328,000feet
Max speed attained	3,500 mph	Weight of explosive	2,000lbs

These two plans were compiled at the end of the war to show the extent of the V1 and V2 offensives on England. They were taken from drawings made by RAF draughtsmen who worked at The Rookery, near Biggin Hill, which was part of "Diver" control.

This excellent example of a flying bomb on its ramp can be found at the Duxford Museum, near Cambridge. After the war, several ramps were brought to Britain for assessment and use in experimental programmes. The ramps were rebuilt and when no longer required, lay abandoned for more than 30 years. A number of sections were brought to Duxford and they were restored and assembled over a period of two years by a team from the Community Programme.

This stained glass window at Staplehurst parish church, Kent was made up of fragments of a previous window which was shattered when a flying bomb landed nearby, on August 8, 1944.

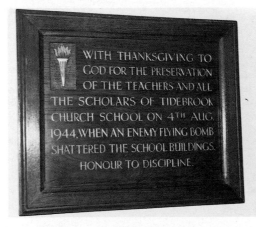

WITH THANKSGIVING TO GOD FOR THE PRESERVATION OF THE TEACHERS AND ALL THE SCHOLARS OF TIDEBROOK CHURCH SCHOOL ON 4TH AUG, 1944, WHEN AN ENEMY FLYING BOMB SHATTERED THE SCHOOL BUILDINGS. HONOUR TO DISCIPLINE.

The plaque in Tidebrook church, near Mayfield, East Sussex reads August 4, 1944. In fact it was August 3 when the village schoolchildren had such a miraculous escape. See page 109.

Launch of a V2 from a field near Wassenaar, The Netherlands during the height of the rocket assault on London. From the first V2, which landed at Chiswick on September 8, 1944 to the one fired on the last day of December, not a single day went by without a launch. The final rocket crashed in Orpington on Tuesday March 27, 1945.

INDEX

This index contains place names and names of the principal characters in the flying bomb campaign which appear in the general text. It does not include the names of the many contributors who responded to our appeal for reminiscences. They have received individual letters of acknowledgement.

Wing Commander Roland Beamont CBE, DSO, DFC, DL commander, in 1944, of the 150 Tempest Wing was the man who led the battle in the air against ther flying bomb. He was one of The Few who fought in the Battle of France, the Battle of Britain and through the war years to the Invasion. On October 12, 1944, Beamont crash-landed his Tempest in Germany and was taken POW. After the war he became a leading Test Pilot, remaining as a highly respected figure in the aviation branch of the Aircraft Industry. He retired from British Aerospace on delivery of the first-production Tornado.

Peter Findley, whose story is told briefly on page 58, has spent more than four years trying to find out more about his mother, Catherine Inwood who was killed when a V1 fell on Weald House, Crockham Hill. His investigations brought him to Edenbridge churchyard where a memorial stone marks the names of those who died in one of the most tragic incidents of all. Peter has met many people who knew his mother vaguely and has received amazing photographs and letters but, by 1992, no relative of his had been found.

There is little evidence today of the destruction wrought by the V-weapons. One exception, however, is the remains of St Mary of the Holy Rood, the church which was destroyed by a flying bomb, shot down by a fighter a few minutes after 8 pm on the evening of Wednesday August 16, 1944. The bomb landed on the tower of the Norman church and six bells came crashing down followed by the walls. Villagers at Little Chart, just south of Charing, campaigned to keep the remains, now covered in ivy, as a symbol of Kent's ordeal in the summer of 1944. A new church, much closer to the village centre, was consecrated in 1958.

Bob Ogley

Bob was a journalist for 30 years until leaving the editorship of *The Sevenoaks Chronicle* in 1989 to become a full-time publisher and author. The overnight success of his first book *In The Wake of The Hurricane*, which became a national bestseller in two editions, launched him into publishing in a most dramatic way.

In 1990, he wrote *Biggin on The Bump*, the *Story of the most Famous Fighter Station in the World*, which received tremendous reviews from national, local and aviation press. The book has raised £12,500 in author's royalties for the RAF Benevolent Fund.

Bob has raised a further £60,000 with the hurricane books for environmental charities and has discovered a supplementary career as speaker to clubs and organisations.

Recently he teamed up with Ian Currie and Mark Davison to research write and publish a series of illustrated county books on the history of the weather. In 1991, *The Kent Weather Book* and *The Sussex Weather Book* were number one county bestsellers.

Froglets Publications Ltd

In the Wake of the Hurricane
(Paperback) ISBN 0 9513019 1 8..£9.95

Surrey in the Hurricane
ISBN 0 9513019 2 6 ....£7.50

London's Hurricane
(Paperback) ISBN 0 9513019 3 4..£4.95
(Hardback) ISBN 0 9513019 8 5..£7.95

Eye on the Hurricane Eastern Counties
(Paperback) ISBN 0 9513019 6 9..£7.95
(Hardback) ISBN 0 9513019 7 7..£11.95

Biggin on the Bump The most famous fighter station in the world
(Paperback) ISBN 1 872337 05 8..£9.95
(Hardback) ISBN 1 872337 10 4..£16.99

The Kent Weather Book
ISBN 1 872337 35 X..£9.95

The Sussex Weather Book
ISBN 1 872337 31 9..£10.99

The Norfolk and Suffolk Weather Book
(Paperback) ISBN 1 872337 99 6..£9.95
(Hardback) ISBN 1 872337 98 8..£16.95

The Hampshire and Isle of Wight Weather Book
ISBN 1 872337 20 1..£9.95

The Berkshire Weather Book
ISBN 1872337 48 1..£9.95

Flying Bombs over England by H.E.Bates.
The lost manuscript.
(Hardback) ISBN 1 872337 04 X..£16.99

Kent at War Bob Ogley's latest best seller
(Paperback) ISBN 1 872337 82 1 ....£10.99
(Hardback) ISBN 1 872 337 49 X..£16.99